T0248150

CLYMA est mort

33 1/3 Global

33 1/3 Global, a series related to but independent from **33 1/3**, takes the format of the original series of short, music-based books and brings the focus to music throughout the world. With initial volumes focusing on Japanese and Brazilian music, the series will also include volumes on the popular music of Australia/Oceania, Europe, Africa, the Middle East, and more.

33 1/3 Japan

Series Editor: Noriko Manabe

Spanning a range of artists and genres – from the 1970s rock of Happy End to technopop band Yellow Magic Orchestra, the Shibuya-kei of Cornelius, classic anime series *Cowboy Bebop,* J-Pop/EDM hybrid Perfume, and vocaloid star Hatsune Miku – 33 1/3 Japan is a series devoted to in-depth examination of Japanese popular music of the twentieth and twenty-first centuries.

Published Titles:

Supercell's *Supercell* by Keisuke Yamada

AKB48 by Patrick W. Galbraith and Jason G. Karlin

Yoko Kanno's *Cowboy Bebop Soundtrack* by Rose Bridges

Perfume's *Game* by Patrick St. Michel

Cornelius's *Fantasma* by Martin Roberts

Joe Hisaishi's *My Neighbor Totoro: Soundtrack* by Kunio Hara

Shonen Knife's *Happy Hour* by Brooke McCorkle

Nenes' *Koza Dabasa* by Henry Johnson

Yuming's *The 14th Moon* by Lasse Lehtonen

Forthcoming Titles:

Yellow Magic Orchestra's *Yellow Magic Orchestra* by Toshiyuki Ohwada

Kohaku utagassen: The Red and White Song Contest by Shelley Brunt

33 1/3 Brazil

Series Editor: Jason Stanyek

Covering the genres of samba, tropicália, rock, hip hop, forró, bossa nova, heavy metal and funk, among others, 33 1/3 Brazil is a series devoted to in-depth examination of the most important Brazilian albums of the twentieth and twenty-first centuries.

Published Titles:

Caetano Veloso's *A Foreign Sound* by Barbara Browning

Tim Maia's *Tim Maia Racional Vols. 1 &2* by Allen Thayer

João Gilberto and Stan Getz's *Getz/Gilberto* by Brian McCann

Gilberto Gil's *Refazenda* by Marc A. Hertzman

Dona Ivone Lara's *Sorriso Negro* by Mila Burns

Milton Nascimento and Lô Borges's *The Corner Club* by Jonathon Grasse

Racionais MCs' *Sobrevivendo no Inferno* by Derek Pardue

Naná Vasconcelos's *Saudades* by Daniel B. Sharp

Chico Buarque's First *Chico Buarque* by Charles A. Perrone

Forthcoming titles:

Jorge Ben Jor's *África Brasil* by Frederick J. Moehn

33 1/3 Europe

Series Editor: Fabian Holt

Spanning a range of artists and genres, 33 1/3 Europe offers engaging accounts of popular and culturally significant albums of Continental Europe and the North Atlantic from the twentieth and twenty-first centuries.

Published Titles:

Darkthrone's *A Blaze in the Northern Sky* by Ross Hagen

Ivo Papazov's *Balkanology* by Carol Silverman

Heiner Müller and Heiner Goebbels's *Wolokolamsker Chaussee* by Philip V. Bohlman

Modeselektor's *Happy Birthday!* by Sean Nye

33 1/3 Oceania

Series Editors: Jon Stratton (senior editor) and Jon Dale (specializing in books on albums from Aotearoa/New Zealand)

Spanning a range of artists and genres from Australian Indigenous artists to Maori and Pasifika artists, from Aotearoa/New Zealand noise music to Australian rock, and including music from Papua and other Pacific islands, 33 1/3 Oceania offers exciting accounts of albums that illustrate the wide range of music made in the Oceania region.

CLYMA est mort

Darren Jorgensen

Series Editors: Jon Stratton, UniSA Creative, University of South
Australia, and Jon Dale, University of Melbourne, Australia

BLOOMSBURY ACADEMIC
NEW YORK • LONDON • OXFORD • NEW DELHI • SYDNEY

BLOOMSBURY ACADEMIC
Bloomsbury Publishing Inc
1385 Broadway, New York, NY 10018, USA
50 Bedford Square, London, WC1B 3DP, UK
29 Earlsfort Terrace, Dublin 2, Ireland

BLOOMSBURY, BLOOMSBURY ACADEMIC and the Diana logo are trademarks of
Bloomsbury Publishing Plc

First published in the United States of America 2023

Copyright © Darren Jorgensen, 2023

For legal purposes the Acknowledgments on p. xi constitute an extension
of this copyright page.

All rights reserved. No part of this publication may be reproduced or transmitted
in any form or by any means, electronic or mechanical, including photocopying,
recording, or any information storage or retrieval system, without prior
permission in writing from the publishers.

Bloomsbury Publishing Inc does not have any control over, or responsibility for, any
third-party websites referred to or in this book. All internet addresses given in this book
were correct at the time of going to press. The author and publisher regret any
inconvenience caused if addresses have changed or sites have ceased to exist,
but can accept no responsibility for any such changes.

Whilst every effort has been made to locate copyright holders the publishers would be
grateful to hear from any person(s) not here acknowledged.

Epigraph used with permission by the Estate of Oleksandr Yevtushenko.

Library of Congress Cataloging-in-Publication Data

Names: Jorgensen, Darren, author.
Title: Clyma est mort / Darren Jorgensen.
Description: [1st.] | New York : Bloomsbury Academic, 2023. | Series: 33 1/3 Oceania |
Includes bibliographical references and index. | Summary: "Discusses improvised rock and
DIY labels stretching from Dunedin, the tiny centre of New Zealand pop and rock, to Europe
and the US through The Dead C's Clyma est mort album" – Provided by publisher.
Identifiers: LCCN 2022055155 (print) | LCCN 2022055156 (ebook) |
ISBN 9781501386954 (hardback) | ISBN 9781501386961 (paperback) | I
SBN 9781501386978 (ebook) | ISBN 9781501386985 (pdf) |
ISBN 9781501386992 (ebook other)
Subjects: LCSH: Dead C (Musical group). Clyma est mort. |
Noise rock (Music)–New Zealand–Dunedin–History and criticism. |
Rock music–New Zealand–Dunedin–1991–2000–History and criticism.
Classification: LCC ML421.D395 J67 2023 (print) | LCC ML421.D395 (ebook) |
DDC 781.66093/9209049—dc23/eng/20221227
LC record available at https://lccn.loc.gov/2022055155
LC ebook record available at https://lccn.loc.gov/2022055156

ISBN: HB: 978-1-5013-8695-4
       PB: 978-1-5013-8696-1
       ePDF: 978-1-5013-8698-5
       eBook: 978-1-5013-8697-8

Typeset by RefineCatch Limited, Bungay, Suffolk
Printed and bound in Great Britain

Series: 33 1/3 Oceania

To find out more about our authors and books visit www.bloomsbury.com
and sign up for our newsletters.

Contents

Acknowledgements

Much of the material in this book comes from interviews with Michael Morley and Bruce Russell, as well as online discussions with Tom Lax, and interviews with Alastair Galbraith, Danny Butt, Graeme Downes, Jane Dodd, Kim Pieters, Nathan Thompson, Richard Ram and Tim Cornelius. I was also privileged to speak to Peter Stapleton and Roy Colbert who are tragically no longer with us. I want to thank everyone for making room for me, especially Bruce for coming through time and time again, and Tom who took all the photographs reproduced here. Anecdotes, gossip and quotes from these interviews are used without footnotes.

This little book would not have happened but for 33 1/3 Oceania co-editor Jon Dale, who was there from its beginnings with his immeasurable knowledge, skills and support. Thanks too to those who helped along the way, especially Malcolm Riddoch and Jo Burzynska, Karl Halliday, Mats Gustafsson, Charles Nielsen of Bananafish, Amanda Mills and Katherine Milburn of the Hocken Collections, and my old friends Simone 'Bid' Nelson, Matt Niedra, Raymond Gristwood and Lach Conn. Some of the ideas in this book were rehearsed in the *Journal of Popular Music Studies*, *Perfect Beat*, *Sound Scripts* and *Writing Around Sound*. Thanks to the editors of these publications, especially Jonathan Marshall of *Sound Scripts*. While writing this I have been employed by the School of Design at the University of Western Australia, who supported my travel with a sabbatical grant and a research committee grant. Finally, thanks to Catherine for letting me take the family stereo into the shed for the duration, and to Akira and Jasper for putting up with endless singalongs in the car.

1 An American Visits New Zealand Only to Find that Nobody Wants to Play

In 1992 Tom Lax arrived in New Zealand lugging a box of The Dead C's just pressed double LP *Harsh 70s Reality* (1992). Lax was running the Siltbreeze label in Philadelphia and had an ear for low-fi, noisy bands who messed with rock in one way or another. He had been enthralled by the records and cassettes arriving from Dunedin, a town famous for indie rock released through the Flying Nun label. The Dead C had put out a couple of records on Flying Nun too, *DR503* (1988) and *Eusa Kills* (1989), but they sounded nothing like the nifty songwriting of The Clean, The Chills, Straitjacket Fits, Tall Dwarfs and The Verlaines, who had brought Flying Nun international attention. Instead, The Dead C were turning drums, guitars, found instruments and amplifiers into charred, noisy topographies. Their loose, downtrodden anarchism was more on the Siltbreeze spectrum of North American bands, such as Mike Rep and the Quotas and V-3. Not that The Dead C sounded much like these bands, either, but were like them less musical, and more interested in generating a racket.

The Dead C came into being in the aftermath of Flying Nun's departure from New Zealand's South Island. *DR503* and

Eusa Kills were released as Flying Nun stumbled into a crisis. Late in 1987 New Zealand's EMI pressing plant, where they had manufactured all their vinyl, closed as CDs promised to be the medium of the future. The rumour was that the record press had been thrown into the sea. Flying Nun boss Roger Shepherd freaked out because it was going to be too costly and time consuming to press vinyl overseas. He made a deal with Australia's WEA label, and then with Mushroom, who had the money to finance a handful of bands to record and tour overseas. In the process Shepherd decided Flying Nun could no longer support the label's less commercially promising acts, in what would prove the beginning of a decline for a label that had traded on its idiosyncratic, independent sounds. They sold out, as the saying goes, moving offices to Auckland in the North Island of the country, becoming part of the complex machinery of a music industry feeding on a new wave of alternative rock.

Let's not be too quick to judge Shepherd. He was only doing what a lot of other smaller labels were doing around the turn of the decade. Smaller labels who had made their own way in the 1980s made these deals after finding themselves with famous acts but not a lot of experience or knowhow to support them. They turned to bigger and more commercially minded operations to help them along. The big music conglomerates were making even more money as they sold CDs at the same price or higher than vinyl records, even though they cost much less to make. Swallowing smaller labels was one way of spending the profits. The devil is always in the details of these deals, however, and by the 1990s the two independent labels that had been luminous examples for Flying Nun, Rough Trade and Slash, were bankrupt and bought out respectively. While today such corporate shenanigans are the normal run of things, at the time there was a sense that independent music was been eaten alive by corporate monsters.

This was the zeitgeist within which The Dead C started playing, recording, and releasing albums. The Flying Nun era was over, and in its place guitarist, songwriter and vocalist Michael Morley came up with the idea of getting together with drummer Robbie Yeats, and Bruce Russell, who at this time was more an enthusiast than a musician. While Yeats had proved himself a whiz at playing odd syncopations in pop band The Verlaines, and Morley was a regular sight on local stages in his duo with Richard Ram, Wreck Small Speakers on Expensive Stereos, Russell had only been on stage a handful of times in the mid-1980s, playing screeching, experimental guitar with an electric razor. Russell was, however, deeply involved in what was going on around him, having briefly worked for Flying Nun before starting the Xpressway label in 1988, which was primarily dedicated to artists that Flying Nun had abandoned on its move to Auckland. Xpressway's releases, mostly cassettes, were designed with a sense of posterity. Russell carefully and meticulously typed the details of musicians, instruments and recording locations onto neat, photocopied covers, to sustain the history of Dunedin music that Flying Nun had put into motion.

Both Siltbreeze and Xpressway released music that didn't aspire to climb the ladder of commercial success, but they were not amateur operations. They were dedicated to documenting the originality of artists Lax and Russell liked. Today Siltbreeze and Xpressway releases from the 1990s are artefacts from a transitional time in independent music. Their artists were not easily defined, often making something between chaos and noise, the charismatic and the simply odd. If nothing else Lax and Russell worked to unearth artists who sounded like no other, to release them on whatever medium they could afford that suited the material, whether cassette, CD or vinyl. Today these albums, mini-albums, seven and twelve inches are evidence that, before the internet, music was not all a marketing campaign by pointy-headed men. Their recordings are a long way from Spotify's algorithms of taste. Rather than likes and plays, they arrived in the letterbox as evidence of a wider community of people who shared your weird sonic interests.

An interest in doing something different, something that sounded like nobody else, was behind The Dead C from the first time they played together. They were always sure to have a tape recorder running, whether a walkman or a borrowed reel-to-reel, before Morley bought his own Tascam porta-studio. You never knew when something happened that was worth releasing. This dedication to getting everything down on tape surprised Yeats when he first jammed with Morley and Russell:

> **R** *DR503* – I met these two freaks and recorded some music that I didn't really know what the fuck was going on …
>
> **M** He was in The Verlaines.
>
> **R** … in a very sunny room on a one-track reel-to-reel tape recorder and it turned out to become a record. Bruce and Michael said, 'hey, we've got an album of this,' and I went, 'What?!'
>
> **M** (*laughs*) You're lying.
>
> **R** No, I'm not lying, Michael, I'm telling the truth. I was sort of tapping my part on a snare drum on the floor, on the carpet, sitting round on this very sunny afternoon, like a Tuesday afternoon. And that went on for about two weeks, as

far as I can remember, and at the end of it they said they had an album, and I could not believe it was the truth, but it was the truth, and that's *DR503*. Then things got pretty sinister.[1]

This getting together and recording things was not done with the aim of perfecting the playing of songs. It was instead to make rough impressions of these get togethers on tape. There is no perfect version, no perfect recording. The price of this kind of recording is that you might hear some instruments or sounds more than others on any particular track. As Joe Tunis notes in a podcast with Rob Elba:

Tunis   I think the aesthetic of the recording style lends a ton to it, like if the drums were mic'd like crazy it wouldn't sound the way it sounds, I think it wouldn't have the feeling that it has.

Elba   Right, it's true it gives it a very found sound quality, almost like all three of them were just sort of found, like someone stumbled across them making noise.

Tunis   Like a tape in a trunk somewhere.

And so, when it comes to hearing the drums or any particular instrument, it can be tricky to tell one from the other, because they aren't separated as they are in a studio recording. On *Trapdoor Fucking EXIT*, Tunis and Elba can't quite work out whether Yeats is playing a full drum kit:

Tunis   I can't tell if he has any other drum but a snare.

Elba   I know, I was wondering is there a kick, but it's just not mic'd, but then I'm thinking no don't think there is.

Tunis   Sometimes you can kind of maybe hear, and you hear some toms, later on.

Elba   Maybe there's toms, some floor toms, but probably not a kick.

Tunis   Yea it's real minimal. But he's like a drummer drummer.

Elba   Is he really? I was wondering that.

Tunis   Yea he played in Verlaines and stuff like that, he knows what he's doing.[2]

Russell also played drums somewhere on *Trapdoor*, confusing this whole discussion of what the drums are doing on this track. The problem, and a constant problem with trying to separate the instruments on any Dead C recording, has to do with the way the band place the recorder in what often sounds like haphazard places around the room. Here the mic is at such a distance from the drums that they do not seem to be picking up the full drum kit although, as Elba and Tunis opine, it is not being played anyway. In every Dead C album recording devices of varying quality mix and mangle the sounds differently, picking up the drums on this track and losing them on another, or creating unintended effects with worn internal mechanisms. Listening back to this ongoing archive, The Dead C would decide some slabs of these recordings sounded better than other slabs, some becoming tracks and some not. When there was enough to go on, a record was in the offing. Morley would come up with cover art, perhaps a linocut or woodcut print, and sometimes a blurry photograph or a weird, classical image from the history of European printmaking.

The Dead C found a niche in the space between New Zealand and the rest of the world. Records were the currency of isolation and recording and releasing records became a way of forging a place within the experimental, rock music underground. The Dead C imagined an audience beyond the Tascam and beyond Dunedin, a crowd produced not by coming together but through distances between individuals, through listening at a distance. This distance is reproduced in The Dead C's sound, as Morley, Russell and Yeats follow their own intuitive bents. For much of the time they are stubbornly in their own corners, throwing musical ideas across the room to see if they add up to something.

Although they had been releasing them since 1981, Flying Nun albums had not flown to North America so quickly. Lax was working in the Philadelphia Record Exchange when he was offered his first batch of Flying Nun albums around 1985 or 1986. British, DIY post-punk was popular at the shop, and Lax would see UK bands after they had arrived on a cheap airline called Laker Airways to do a round of venues in Boston, New York, Philadelphia and Washington. Paisley pop from Los Angeles was on rotation, as were the hipper versions of Australian pub rock, such as Sunnyboys, Died Pretty, New Christs and the Lime Spiders. Nobody had heard much from New Zealand until the distributors at Rough Trade began arriving with kooky-looking Flying Nun albums under their arms. Lax remembers getting the delivery, putting them aside and heading to the pub for a few beers after work. Then, when sufficiently relaxed, venturing back to the shop to hear what they had in stock:

> As the records began to come out of the box, one by one, we were all blown away by what we were seeing. These things looked amazing! The jackets so vibrant & all the labels looked handmade & unique. And of course the music, which was singular in every way.[3]

Discovering Flying Nun 'was like a Renaissance to us', Lax recalls, and not just because of the better-remembered acts of the era, as they played Max Block, The Puddle, The Axemen, and DoubleHappys at the shop. These acts shared something of a live quality that he recognized from the north-east American scene, recordings that came out of intense gigging and with a do-it-yourself quality that stuck its nose up at the high-end production of commercial records.

Lax was enthusiastic about *DR503* when it arrived. It had the laidback quality of Morley's earlier band, Wreck Small Speakers on Expensive Stereos, whose 12-inch *River Falling Love* (1987) had arrived in Philly the year before, but with an edgy, rock intensity that spoke to Lax's taste for DIY, garage sounds. Lax was very keen to contact The Dead C, because he understood that Russell was running Xpressway. He was in luck when a reformed Clean toured North America, and Lax was able to ask Hamish Kilgour for Xpressway's address. Kilgour dutifully sent it to him on a piece of paper. Only then was Lax able to contact Russell. He had attempted to correspond with Flying Nun before this, and not had much more than a catalogue in reply. Russell would have a lot more to say to Lax after his Philadelphia letter was intercepted by a dutiful, New Zealand customs agent. While North American readers among you might be used to living with cocaine, guns and extreme pornography, such things are harder to come by in the pastoral arcadia of the south. Included in Lax's letter was a copy of his *Siltbreeze* zine, an A5, badly photocopied and stapled publication in which he'd reviewed *DR503*. This was not an ordinary fanzine, with reviews collaged amongst the most offensive kinds of porn to illustrate Lax's opinions. Russell describes it as 'only the worst inbred redneck ugly obnoxious pornography, ugly people doing ugly things'.[4] He was right to be grumpy, since New

Zealand customs kept an eye on Russell's packages and letters for a couple of years afterward. This was when he was trying to run Xpressway, importing and exporting records without attracting too much attention. A couple of years later customs came to visit Russell again after intercepting something that looked like an acid blotter but was actually a lovely piece of paper wrapping a cheque. Such episodes dot the history of relations between New Zealand labels and New Zealand customs. Flying Nun was also raided by the police after one of their artists sent another some hash through the mail.[5]

After hearing *DR503*, Lax thought he could help by finding The Dead C a North American label. The people he thought would be interested were not, leaving Lax to put out *Helen Said This/Bury* (1990) himself.[6] It was at this point, with this second release, that Lax realised he had started Siltbreeze the label, and he would go on to put out eleven Dead C releases over the next seven years, in a run that represents much of the first period of the band's life. Lax's insight that The Dead C had something that North America would be interested in would come to define the band, who joked that they were more a Philadelphia band than a New Zealand one, as people there had at least heard of them. This is less a joke than it may at first appear; Philly was full of music geeks during the 1990s, who fostered a psychedelic, art rock scene.

After arriving in New Zealand in 1992, Lax stayed with The Dead C for six weeks. He expected that he would see them play live during this time, and perhaps one of the other Dunedin acts he was releasing on Siltbreeze, such as Alastair Galbraith, Queen Meanie Puss, or Morley's solo act, Gate. Surely somebody was going to play at one of the local venues, like they did in North America where there was always a gig around the corner. Eighteen years later, Lax remembers the frustration in 'Cowbell need not apply', an essay describing the making of *Clyma est mort* (1992):

> Outstanding, this was truly going to be the trip of a lifetime. I envisioned a Dead C concert (perhaps a record release party) or better yet, a showcase of Xpressway artists – Dead C, Terminals, Plagal Grind, Sferic Experiment – all playing for ME. Captain America was in town and he was putting them on the map. I figured any and all would be only too happy to perform, a small token for all the enthusiasm, hard work and money I'd surrendered.
>
> But I figured wrong. The days turned into weeks and not a goddamn thing happened –musically. Sure, I was still having a ball, but what the hell? What about something at Alastair Galbraith's space? Or the legendary Chippendale House? Nope. Nada. It wasn't gonna happen. Was I disappointed? Fuck, yes! But the way everyone there felt, organizing something at such a late date (by now, near the end of April) was impossible, and besides, what's the sense of playing live when only one person was interested (Xpressway love at the local level being something of an oxymoron)? I believe out of sheer guilt, Dead C agreed to hold a practice for me at Grey Street (a large ramshackle house and residence where a front room functioned as a rehearsal space) and sometime between that decision and the actual event a plan was hatched to reinvent said rehearsal into a live concert.[7]

Dunedin was not Philadelphia. Its small population was more interested in what was on television and who was winning the rugby. The number of people making and seeing live music could be counted on a few hands. In 1992 there was no appetite among the handful of people to play to an empty venue even if Lax was in it.

The live gig scene had also waned since the heyday of the Flying Nun in the 1980s, when a culture of intensive gigging and songwriting had turned the Empire Tavern into the CBGB's of the Southern Hemisphere. In place of this fulcrum of creativity was a more cynical wisdom that came from the stories of bands who had travelled overseas and come home burned out and broke. Rather than being 'in the vanguard of something', as Shepherd has recently written of The Dead C, the band felt like most of the town really didn't like them, as they did nothing to revive the local culture of making pop music.[8] Even their good friend and Straitjacket Fits singer and songwriter Shayne Carter did not want his name on the liner notes to *Harsh 70s Reality*, where he played on the track Driver U.F.O.. He only admitted in his recent book *Dead People I Have Known* that he 'thought the Dead C were terrible when I first heard them in the early nineties'.[9]

After weeks of Lax harassing them, The Dead C came up with a cheeky plan to keep Lax happy, and to send him back with a new album in his luggage. If he wanted a gig they would give him one, although he would be the only one to see it, and make a live record in the process. *Clyma* was recorded in the front room of Morley's shared house in Grey Street, Port Chalmers, the shipping harbour some fifteen minutes' drive along the coast from Dunedin proper. While Dunedin is almost at the end of the world, Port Chalmers really is at the end of all things. Here the sound of trucks delivering frozen fish, lamb and milk powder can be heard at all hours, most of it bound for China. The main street runs down the hill to the coast and is typically barren of life, its doors closed except for a couple of pubs and restaurants that are barely open. In the 1990s it was not the safest place, with locals and sailors getting into the occasional fisticuffs. By now, most other towns in the Western world would have gentrified this area into a café strip, but even today Port Chalmers feels like a forgotten film set, its facades abandoned for a better class of movie.

The *Clyma* session extended over the last weekend Lax was in Dunedin, before they rushed the cassette tape to Fish St Studio on Sunday night, mastering it onto quarter-inch reels that Lax took back to Philadelphia the next day. *Clyma* follows *Harsh 70s Reality*, the double LP that Siltbreeze had just pressed, an album many still think of as their masterpiece. And yet I hope after reading this book you will agree that *Clyma*, made on a whim over a weekend, is more than a match for *Harsh 70s*, not only because of some seriously brilliant tracks, but because it opens a creaky old door to thinking about the mechanisms of making a rock album. Comparisons that smart people have made between *Harsh 70s* and Royal Trux's double LP *Twin Infinitives* (1990) are in search of some key to The Dead C's *oeuvre*, when their albums are better understood as an ongoing project.[10] Subsequent Royal Trux albums turned into other kinds of rock music, leaving *Twin Infinitives* as a one off. Better North American comparisons are with the overlapping, unceasing intensity of Harry Pussy, Sun City Girls or the improvising collective No-Neck Blues Band, whose signature intensities can be instantly recognized because they overlap from album to album.

The Dead C had spent two years making *Harsh 70s,* doing a lot of curating in the selection of tracks and post-production, but were soon to discover, in the recording of *Clyma*, that they did not need to put as much effort into making a record. And the kicker is that an album recorded quickly can be just as good as a much-worked-on record, the live record made on a whim as good as the heavily curated one. The band had already discovered that they didn't need a big studio with which to make a record. They didn't even need a very long set of songs. *Clyma* forces us to rethink the reasons that we think of one album as being better than another. As Lax recalls after driving from Port Chalmers to the Fish Street Studios in Dunedin for mastering, the session had 'inexplicably transformed itself into a bloody fantastic LP'.[11] The magic lay not in the perfection of the playing of songs, nor the chance synchrony of a group improvization, but in the way that they had come to know how to play alongside each other. With *Clyma*, the albums come to represent a new confidence in playing and releasing whatever was working for the band at the time. It's what fellow Port Chalmers musician Peter Stapleton described as 'audio verite', a philosophy of playing and releasing music unencumbered by the kinds of expectations that people put on themselves and each other to make good albums rather than bad ones; to be serious musicians rather than simply having a good time.

While *Clyma* confuses our categories of the live and studio album, as well as the serious album and the throwaway joke, it is also the moment in which The Dead C begin to confuse the improvization and the song. Mixing up both, in tracks that veer into and out of the song form, *Clyma* confuses our expectations of what we are supposed to be listening to when we listen to a rock record, throwing up questions about the way bands do things and what they are expected to do. In the years after *Clyma*, The Dead C would throw off the constraints of the rehearsed song entirely, just as from their very beginnings they had abandoned the idea of recording albums in a studio. Songs would instead appear amidst long improvised sessions, made up on the spot, brought into being by an accidental coincidence of riffs, rhythms and sometimes vocals. As the 1990s wore on, The Dead C grew in their confidence to do whatever they liked on stage and off, making slow, broody atmospheres as readily as riffing into Morley's desultory lyrics and Yeats's unpredictable beat. Out of the chaotic nothingness comes something, but this something is always about to dissolve, the ear suspended between one kind of listening and another.

This shapeshifting is there from the first track on *Clyma*, 'Sunshine-Dirt for Harry'. There are two titles because the track shifts from a moody combination of warbling, guitar noodling and a muted sample into a song and then into a speedy instrumental finale. 'Sunshine-Dirt for Harry' sets the mood for *Clyma* as it mashes a brooding melancholia of noise into riff-oriented rock music. Not that everyone in the band is on board this shift from one to the other, as what first seems to be coalescing into a song is postponed for some minutes by Russell's distracted attention to a drawl of feedback through his amplifier. Screeching turns into blaring that gives way to Morley making a downward-facing riff and lyrics to suit.

While bands are always the sound of everyone working together, 'Sunshine-Dirt for Harry' illustrates the way that, in The Dead C at least, individuals are never subservient to the whole, as Morley, Russell and Yeats work against each other by using their instruments as devices for making noise, interrupting each other as much as flowing into whatever overall design might be emerging from the mess. Yeats drives the changes from moody improvization to song to a concluding, noisy jam as he kicks in with different drum riffs, compelling the other two not to get too comfortable. The track is a Brechtian beginning to *Clyma*, as The Dead C play out their philosophy of recording whatever they are doing, and doing what they feel like, in the process illustrating the way albums are not clean commodities but come out of people sitting amidst a mess of plugs and wires.

The track also illustrates the way they play against rather than with each other. They perform this very tension in interviews, too, contradicting and disagreeing with whatever the others might say:

d   You react to/against and feed off Michael?

B   Oh yeah, definitely, even when he's not playing notes and chords or indeed playing anything at all. (*laughter*) We have a relationship outside of just what we do in music, and I think it's reflected in what we do. That's why I always try and do whatever he doesn't.

d   What you're doing seems completely unrelated to what he's doing.

M   Yeah.

R   Do you think so?

M   *Yeah.*

R   Oh crap. I resent that, I think they're exactly complementary.

M   Overall, maybe it is. But at the time you're thinking of things that are gonna throw each other off.

B   Definitely. There is a combative aspect. (laughter)

R   *Combative?*

B   Yeah. Life is a battle. Didn't Pat Benatar tell us that?[12]

While Morley (M) and Russell (B) agree that they disrupt each other's playing, Yeats (R) disagrees with the two of them.

We know the song that the first track on *Clyma* kicks into is called 'Sunshine' because it also appears on a Gate seven inch that was also released in 1992, *Sunshine/Ives*. Gate is the name for Morley's various sonic experiments and a small mountain of releases. At first glance, The Dead C turning up on a Gate release appears to be something of a drunken moment in Morley's trajectory, but the two versions also illuminate the blurred lines between his own songwriting and The Dead C's activities, at least in these early years of the band. If anything, the confusion of Morley's releases illustrates his incredible productivity, as he released two full-length Gate LPs in 1992, *Guitar* and *Metric*, both on Seattle's Majora label. In addition, there are three seven inches from 1992, including *Sunshine/Ives*, the brilliant *Prophet/Rebel* in Siltbreeze whose gothic electronica works at both 33 and 45 rpm, and the *Islands of Memory* lathe cut.

'Sunshine' appears on *Clyma* as if by chance, as about three minutes into the track it sounds like Morley and Russell have decided they like the combination of an almost ambient, amplified hum (Russell) and a twangy, deep guitar riff (Morley). Yeats comes into the mix, pulling a steady, low rumble of drums out of nowhere to build the atmosphere, before Morley begins singing, so that we know that we have somehow arrived amidst a song,

> Cast away
> Cast away from harm, hilltop
> And far away
> And I'm going two ways now
> Can this be? Can this be?
> And I'm not thinking towards it
> Roll over now my arm's asleep
> Feels talked about, well understood
> Roll over now

Take a look and see
Take a look and see
Can't do nothing wrong now

Heavy metal guitar shows, 3D amp
The way the media represent male and female
Tom Hanks and his dog
Moving, through
Shave your legs
Shave your arms
Today I felt a lot closer
Today I got a lot better
I want to send a letter
and I want to ring
I want to even talk
(there's an undecipherable lyric here)
I just don't know

Morley is 'far away' before he 'felt a lot closer', thinking about sending letters and talking on the phone, playing out that Dead C motif of distance in his lyrics. The 3D amp may well be a reference to the 3Ds, who Morley and Yeats played with in Auckland in 1989. And that his arm has gone to sleep while watching Tom Hanks in *Turner and Hooch* (1989) on late-night television. The Gate version of this track has different lyrics, ending 'Take a look and see', giving us some insight into the way in which Morley is winging it as he goes along, that 'Sunshine' has no pre-existing version, but ones that vaguely come and vaguely go after the whims of the band.

It is not long into *Clyma*, and not long into the beautiful, sinking vessel of 'Sunshine' that Morley's vocals are swallowed

Figure 1 *Morley on guitar and Yeats on drums playing in the Clyma sessions. Photo Tom Lax.*

up by a new volume of Russell's arcing feedback. Yeats has already shifted the drum rhythm away from the more sedate backing he was giving Morley, before being gripped by inspiration to play loud and fast, and into another, more jagged track that is presumably 'Dirt for Harry.' The band turns everything around and into a completely different mood to the one that came before, Morley shaking a guitar back into Yeats's increasingly frenetic drumming. It is a shock when, with some synchrony with each other, Morley, Russell and Yeats seem to know how and when to tune down and end the track. The song disintegrates, in a characteristically punchy outro.

The way that 'Sunshine' is quickly overtaken by other sounds sets up a spectre of dissolution that hangs over the *Clyma* record, its riffs threatened with a chaos in which there is no structure at all for the listener to hang onto. The compelling aspect of these improvizations, and an aspect of all Dead C recordings, is that their noises are never vague, but are deliberate and compulsively made, the will of the musicians blasting against each other. It may be better to think of 'Sunshine-Dirt for Harry' as a collage rather than as a song or a blend of song and improvization. It is a collage in which Morley, Russell and Yeats push at each other, overlapping each other's sonics and playing their own thing while also coming together, before pulling apart once more.

2 You Wouldn't Play Like that if You Didn't Know What You Were Doing[1]

The Dead C's distinct sound was there from the band's very first moments playing together. Their first cassette release, *The Dead See Perform Max Harris* from 1987 (re-released on vinyl in 2010), documents their second-ever rehearsal, the first side recorded onto a Walkman and the second onto a reel-to-reel loaned to the band by Dunedin musician Peter Gutteridge, with Yeats playing boxes and pots. This all took place in Francisca Griffin's living room (Griffin played with Flying Nun band Look Blue Go Purple under the name Kathy Bull). After hearing their second record, *DR503*, on vinyl the band decided that the low-fi quality of cassette recording was their preferred method of making a record. It's good to remember the cassette was not the maligned media it would become in the era of the CD. Cassette releases in North America, the UK and on Flying Nun in New Zealand were an important part of independent music. The Dead C were also very inspired by Captain Beefheart and his Magic Band's *Trout Mask Replica* (1969), some of which was made, field recording style, on a cassette recorder at Frank Zappa's house.

The cassette would triumph over the studio in The Dead C's methods after they heard the vinyl pressing of *DR503*. Half of this record was recorded onto cassette porta-studio, and it was this half that they preferred. The other half, 'Max', 'Mutterline', 'Polio' and '3 Years', was recorded on an 8-track at the local university radio station. Russell got carried away with the equipment on 'Mutterline', collaging cassette samples atop a band recording to make a mashed-up version of The Dead C, that feels bewildered rather than having the raw confidence of much of the band's early sound. 'Mutterline' is, however, the first more experimental song released by The Dead C, the track in which found instruments play a leading role for the first time= and in which they indulge an interest in making deconstructive noise. Costing NZ$200, this studio session that makes up half of *DR503* remains the most expensive recording The Dead C ever made.

This aversion to the recording studio rejects an assumption on the part of bands and music industry alike that cleaned up studio recordings are better than rough ones. Studios that separate instruments from each other do not, after all, resemble the way that bands play along with each other. Musicians do not separate out into different rooms and face different microphones when they are rehearsing or jamming, to be remixed by someone in yet another room, fiddling with buttons and knobs. They work in sight and sound of each other, all the better to make things work together. The Dead C's use of a low fidelity Tascam is more like a field recording than a studio or live recording technique. The microphone is placed where it might capture the best possible portrait of the room they are playing in.

The Dead C didn't need an expensive studio or a star producer that other New Zealand bands had been using, to make a record they were happy with. As Yeats points out, speaking about recording *Eusa Kills* in Alastair Galbraith's warehouse,

Mr. Yeats   You know, you can pay $1,500 a day to hire a DBX bloody reverb or whatever …"

Mr. Russell   Or you can go to Alastair's for nothing.

Mr. Yeats   And get a hell of a lot more natural reverb, with big wooden walls …[2]

Russell is also fond of reminding interviewers that he could barely play guitar when he joined The Dead C, and still can't play it in any kind of conventional way. He remembers Morley saying, '"Max Harris", and I would furiously think oh, that's the one where I had my fingers here and here and we would just play it, making it up as we went along.' Later, when Russell collaborated with Alastair Galbraith on long improvizational records as *A Handful of Dust*, Russell would pull a similar trick. Galbraith asks us to imagine,

> What it feels like to perform live with no idea at all of what you are about to do, or what your fellow band member will do? To be told: 'This next piece will be called The Kabbalah of the horse pegasus.'[3]

Morley remembers in these first years of The Dead C that,

> I wouldn't say we were writing songs but I would come to the band with ideas on the guitar and some lyrics and they would be presented and they would just play along. Maybe if they could remember what we were doing, you know, each time we had a song. But it got to a point that it was pointless. I don't see the point in writing songs and repeating these songs over and over again. That's the thing that I got quite anxious about. When you see bands you admire and they get

up on stage and they play their album, and you think what about some of their other songs, why aren't they playing anything else, well they haven't prepared for those ones, they haven't rehearsed them. And you think, oh my god! Rehearsed? Why can't they just play them roughly?

As a songwriter, Morley had the most to lose by being in The Dead C. He talks about what it might have meant to be writing songs, looking back upon the labyrinth of life choices that would have meant he played in a more conventional band. Yet, he thinks, this would have turned him into a different kind of person and he and The Dead C were familiar enough with the rock-star complexes that had arisen around Dunedin to know that this is not what they wanted for themselves.[4]

Versions of half of the songs on *Clyma*, including 'Sunshine', can be found on other cassettes, CDs, singles and LPs. The other tracks are not so much songs as improvised dirges, made up on the spot in the front room of Russell's shared house. The album realises The Dead C's philosophy of playing, recording everything and taking what you think sounds good to make a record. If you veer into making a song while playing, all well and good. If not, you are 'jamming' as rock musicians might put it or doing 'free improvization' as jazz musicians say. These terms are so loaded, however, by dint of being opposed to playing songs or compositions, that they do not quite capture the kind of freedom that comes with recording everything. As we now know, too, improvization is something of a myth when it comes to describing the original free jazz of the 1960s and 1970s. These records were post-produced and designed by visionaries such as Ornette Coleman and Miles Davis rather than being particularly free. These studio sessions were also incredibly expensive, putting pressure on musicians in a way that has little in common with the cassette recording techniques of The Dead C. Like these jazz musicians, however, there is something of a discipline at work in the way The Dead C play together, the concentrated effort of a correspondence between Yeats, Russell and Morley, in a conversation that runs between albums. After all, by the time of *Clyma*, they had been playing together for five years.

Their musical conversation does not settle down into too much of a groove, partly because the band decided, after The Cramps and The DoubleHappys, to do without a bass guitarist. This is also because Yeats chops and changes The Dead C's drum rhythms to avoid catching the ear with a bad infinity of repetition. He speeds up and slows down as he feels like it, and sabotages synchrony by switching rhythms. His shifts will turn the total sound into something else, another form of relation between instruments, interrupting what we thought was a flow of musicality. 'The trip is everything', says Russell, 'Most

Figure 2 *Russell playing the amplifier for* Clyma. *Photo Tom Lax.*

stable structure'. There's an anarchist idea of the song here, as three individuals come together and do what they like, and do it with each other, to make a series of tracks that makes up an album. The joy of the sound is to hear a chaotic arrangement come together somehow, to cohere into something more than the sum of its individual parts, and yet remain a conversation of these parts that remain stubbornly themselves.

Russell is the philosopher in the group, writing for *The Wire* magazine among other publications, and it is through his writing that it is possible to think through some of The Dead C's approach to playing. His early ideas on sound include the now iconic 'What is Free? A Free Noise Manifesto,' that can be read as an early attempt to defend their approach against the weight of Dunedin's historic interest in the singer-songwriter.[5] 'What is Free?' was not only a defence of The Dead C, but also other acts playing and recording in Dunedin at the time, including collaborations that Morley and Russell had with other musicians. It was also a way for Russell to explain his approach to guitar, his inability to play guitar and yet to make it work somehow with an amplifier and whatever he found to scratch on its strings. 'What is Free?' is, however, an obscure justification, drawing upon Russell's extensive reading, and his understanding of avant-garde music, mixed in with quotes from the Renaissance occultist Robert Fludd and the philosopher Ludwig Wittgenstein. The 1960s opened a portal, he writes, as the experimental music of La Monte Young, Lou Reed, Karl Stockhausen and free jazz revolutionized music before academicism and the market cartels 'papered over' and 'crushed the zone of discontinuity'. Part of the plea for 'Free Noise' is for the special role that technology plays in liberating musician and sound alike:

8. Noise from amplified electrical instruments, especially from defective and/or 'low tech' equipment, opens immense areas of the audible frequency spectrum to exploitation by the Free musician.

8.1) The medium is (a part of) the message.

8.2) Broken machines distance the musician from the process of music. In this way random factors are introduced, analogous to those which arise from the interplay of harmonic overtones in an acoustic environment (a factor in a later stage of the music process).

8.3) Form and content come together in an apparent vacuity. The mode of recording is a part of the process, and an integral part of the outcome. The artificial distinction between musician (Artist) and technician (Craftsman) is dissolved.

9. Free music which utilizes rock instrumentation and aesthetics as its jumping-off point can harness a noise more purely random and less limited by subjective considerations than that of any but the most determined acoustic musicians.

The defensive tone to Russell's writing shifts from highly regarded, avant-garde composers to claiming space for amplifiers and pedals in their lineage. It's an argument for the democratizing effects of technology rather than artists. After all, The Dead C were not living in New York, where specialized scenes of art, music and film sustain themselves over generations of artists. Neither were they in London, where the big names of improvised music gathered to push boundaries only known to themselves.

The publication history of 'What is Free?' illustrates something of the internationalism of which The Dead C were a part during the 1990s. An early draft appeared in the liner notes for Morley's lathe cut *Islands of Memory* from 1992, released in an edition of twenty in the year of *Clyma*'s release. The covers of these seven inches were encrusted with dirt and leaves and shown on the floor of an art gallery at an exhibition of the same name, while synthesizers plugged into an amplifier made a horrific noise for the duration of the exhibition. Suffice to say that nobody in Dunedin bought the records, which Morley mostly gave away, but the entirety of a second pressing was bought by the Boston-based Forced Exposure label, as part of an international fascination with a new wave of Dunedin music. There's a record of 'What is Free?' being published in *Snafu*, a zine that has disappeared into the abyss of time, but it got a wider readership when it was printed alongside a cheesy picture of kids wearing headphones in San Francisco's *Bananafish* magazine in 1993. Photocopies of this copy were printed, circulated, and copied and circulated again. 'What is Free?' was also printed in Russell's *Logopandocy: The Journal of Vain Erudition* mini-zine that came with the Handful of Dust album *Musica Humana* from 1994, a compilation of tracks from Russell's esoteric collaboration with Galbraith, and finally in a collection of Russell's writing called *Left-Handed Blows* in 2009. In later years Russell replaced free noise with 'improvisational musical practice', 'Improvised Sound Work (ISW)' and 'mis-competence' to explain something of what was taking place around him.[6]

Mis-competence is an 'ability to do something both deliberately wrongly, and well', precisely describing Russell's own disciplined spontaneity, and the liminal zone that he carves out with a screeching amplifier.[7] Mis-competence frames not only his own practice, but also that of anyone who might find an unconventional sound compelling to listen to and follows that sound to make something new. The mis-competent are a stubborn sort of musician, who make and record sound with little concern for how it fits into a properly musical context. It describes artists that Russell would come to release later in the 1990s on his second label, Corpus Hermeticum (Hermescorp). Doramaar, Omit, the Sandoz Lab Technicians and The Shadow Ring were non-musicians finding their way to recording albums that sounded like no other.

With Hermescorp, Russell shifted from the cassettes that defined Xpressway to bespoke, neatly designed CDs. After Morley had told him how cheap CDs were to produce, Russell crafted paper and cardboard covers and zines to go with them, selling them via mail order across the seas. Russell had moved from Port Chalmers to Lyttelton, the port of Christchurch a few hundred kilometers to the north. Moving from one port to another, Russell was once again close to the shipping routes and the feeling of internationalism they produce. The first ten Hermescorp releases, carefully packaged and posted to Europe, North America, Japan and Australia, were of Russell's own projects, mostly his collaboration with Galbraith and Stapleton, A Handful of Dust. While mis-competence is a more particular concept, 'free noise' has become a way of describing a more widespread interest in improvisation, especially this body of releases from both Russell and another Port Chalmers label, Metonymic. Stapleton was the innovator and organizer behind Metonymic, who released improvised albums made with his then partner and artist Kim Pieters. Rain (Danny Butt, Pieters, Stapleton), Flies Inside the Sun (Butt, Brian Crook, Pieters, Stapleton), Sleep (Pieters, Nathan Thompson, Stapleton, Susan Ballard) and Pieters/Russell/Stapleton all recorded albums in a house in Pūrākaunui, on a hill above Port Chalmers. This free noise movement has a distinctly New Zealand aesthetic, with minimal, cardboard covers reflecting a do-it-yourself ethos behind recording and releasing. Hermescorp and Metonymic testify to the antipathy to convention contained by the concept of free noise, combining it with an enthusiasm for the possibilities of playing and recording the previously unheard.

3 In Which the Band Find Themselves in Front of the Whole Country

The second track on *Clyma* is 'Sky', a song that had various incarnations in the early years of The Dead C. It was the song they played to a national audience when they appeared on the soon-to-be-canned music show 'Ground Zero' on New Zealand television in 1999. In a tight three-minute slot that left no room to build a mood they rush into a blare of noise; Morley and Russell dressed up in suits while Yeats mustn't have got the memo. Russell steals the show with a series of antics with his guitar, first waving it frantically into the microphone, then putting an electric fan onto it, and then sitting it on top of the amp to scratch at its strings with a pair of toy sticks. Amidst the havoc Morley can be heard yelling, 'Rented my arse to see the sky', as if this is happening here and now in the suit he is wearing on live television, yet. in the process. they turn the television into another noise machine, making a pointedly punk spectacle out of the little time they have been given, and would never be given again. It's difficult to believe that nothing gets destroyed in the madness, before the whole spectacle stops suddenly and a couple of blonde boys try to say something nice about it while looking utterly bemused.

In a following segment Ground Zero presenter and Able Tasmans vocalist Graeme Humphreys has them on a couch to ask about CD re-releases of Alan Vega and Martin Rev's duo

Suicide which he had just received in the post. It's a thin piece of television, and completely bewildering as to why Humphreys is talking about Suicide rather than interviewing The Dead C. Russell rises to the occasion and demonstrates a vinylophilic knowledge of both Suicide and their re-releases while puffing on a big cigar. Morley looks on with typical charisma, while Yeats looks completely bored.

While it is impossible to hear much of Morley's vocals on the television broadcast, they rise above the fast blasts of drums and guitar on *Clyma*'s version of 'Sky'. He must have been standing close to the microphone. Like a double haiku, the lyrics ring clearly atop the whole rocking blare, staying with the listener after the noise comes to an end:

> Rented my arse
> to see the sky
> Rented my arse
> to see the sky
> You dumb fucks
> don't mean very much
> I've got more important things
> to worry about.

If Morley is referring to his own arse in the first part of the lyric, by the second he has decided he has had enough, and gets on with other, unnamed things that we are not privy to. Let's face it, we are probably the 'dumb fucks' he is singing about.

'Sky' was The Dead C's choice on this television program as it is the track that can be played loudest, most frenetically and to most effect amidst the ambience of a music television programme. The blistering performance is as close as you could come to interrupting the usual run of band fodder. 'Sky' also interrupts the flow of the three Dead C records on which it has appeared. On *Clyma* it comes after the lengthy, shifting enigma of 'Sunshine-Dirt for Harry'. On *Harsh 70s Reality* 'Sky' introduces the second side of the vinyl record, and follows the twenty-two-minute epic 'Driver U.F.O.'. On *Trapdoor Fucking EXIT* from 1990 and 1993, 'Sky' breaks up the melancholy with its furious drumming and vocals. In all of these versions there is an unspoken agreement that they will all chew down on their instruments for two or three minutes. The difference on *Trapdoor* is that Chris Heazlewood (of King Loser, Olla and Sferic Experiment) has joined the band on guitar for about half the album, including 'Sky', and this added instrument will provide a more coherent overall sound to the band. While the magic of other albums lies in an unlikely triptych of the three players, Heazlewood pushes The Dead C to the edge of guitar fuzz, 'Sky' becoming more of a rock song than it usually is, threatening to turn The Dead C into a band like any other. This is why *Trapdoor* is something of an outlier in The Dead C's discography, as an extra guitar blurs the tension between the triad that usually defines the band's sound.

'Sky's' various incarnations warn us that without ever using a studio to track and dub, there is no pristine version of this or any other Dead C song. There is, instead, a reworking and a reworking again of a musical form, a return to the idea rather than to some playbook, and as The Dead C go on, an unravelling of the song to extinction. Rambling guitars, the different intonations of Morley's voice and changes in the pace of Yeats's drumming work deconstruct it rather than build the song's identity. The same can be said of the other, classic Dead C track on *Clyma* that is a version of several others, 'Power'. This was first released on *Trapdoor*, the album that ghosts *Clyma*. While *Trapdoor*'s 'Power' offers a clear picture of Morley's vision of life in the aftermath of disaster, this version is slower, emphasizing the movement of guitars from a slow, deep riff into a more frenzied chiming. Along with 'Sky', 'Power' anchors *Clyma* to The Dead C's previous recordings, giving us a sense that this is, in fact, a live album, replaying classic and familiar tracks in newly disordered ways. The difference here lies purely in the way The Dead C's playroom was arranged that day, in the ways that Morley and Russell are facing, and in the way this ordering reveals new relationships between instruments and vocals.

'Power' is the track with the most versions released by The Dead C, from its place on *Clyma* and *Trapdoor* to the first side of the 1991 seven-inch *Mighty/Power/Peace*. While 'Power's' lyrics are about the US invasion of Panama that took place in late 1989/early 1990, the cover photograph of *Mighty/Power/Peace* features a Palestinian protestor making a V for victory sign, his head wrapped in a keffiyeh. Yet another version is released on another single in 2006, *Relax Fallujah-Hell has come*, featuring this same photograph on the cover and, on the rear, a more recent image of US imperialism, showing Marines executing wounded fighters in a Fallujah mosque. The shift from Palestine to Panama to Iraq illustrates an anti-US imperialism trope in Dead C covers and titles, including *Eusa Kills* (1989) and *The White House* (1995). It's not just the US, however. A photograph from the 1968 Soviet invasion of Czechoslovakia appears on the cover of the 2012 album *Armed Courage*. When they appear on record covers, such images become part of a broader history of revolt, as blurred, running figures and arms throwing stones become symbols of an ongoing resistance to political order. Russell writes of this kind of resistance in Situationist terms, in making improvised, chaotic sound, he wants to foster a consciousness that puts cracks in the prevailing order.[1] There is a desire to disturb what the Situationist theorist Guy Debord called the 'spectacle' of the prevailing order, the capitalist illusion that, in *Clyma*'s case, is the order of rock music in the throes of a corporate, money-making machine.[2]

Morley has been the one naming these albums and choosing The Dead C's cover art, while Shepherd remembers Russell turning up to work at Flying Nun in 1987 in 'a Sandinista T-shirt and a Palestinian scarf'. A video of a Dead C gig at the Chippendale House warehouse shows him in a red beret, long a symbol of leftist militancy.[3] Slightly older than Morley and Yeats, Russell was also on the ground during the 1981 protests against the South African rugby tour of New Zealand. This was something of a turning point in the country, as most of the world were refusing tours by South African teams because of apartheid policies that gave blacks, coloured, and whites different rights. The only other country to accept the Springboks team was the United States, where games were played in secret to escape protestors.

It is sometimes said that the 1980s were the 1960s for New Zealand because of the Springboks protests, but the pleasures of the counterculture had arrived long before this. LSD-inspired head parties were taking place all over the country during the 1970s, including in Dunedin where psychiatrists had sparked an interest in the drug by conducting acid tests with samples posted from the Sandoz laboratory.[4] In Dunedin the biggest parties took place in the grounds of Larnach Castle, built a short way from town by a local politician in the nineteenth century. The New Zealand police were way behind the curve on the use of LSD and were simply not aware of the amount of drugs being taken at these events. Music critic and champion of Dunedin's 1980s music Roy Colbert remembers that while they were good parties for the time, the music at the Larnach

Castle gigs was insufferable, as bands played hour-long versions of Traffic's 'Dear Mr. Fantasy'.

Russell has used the idea of the psychedelic to describe the early 1980s music scene, summarizing it in the liner notes for the 2012 compilation *Time to Go: The Southern Psychedelic Movement*.[5] Released on a revived Flying Nun label that had been bought back by Roger Shepherd after a couple of decades being run by corporates, *Time To Go* features less-well-known tracks from well-known Dunedin bands to make the argument that the 1980s were the South Island's 1960s. Much of the music that Flying Nun bands were making at the time was influenced by North American acts of the 1960s.

This was also one of the points Colbert made repeatedly in his weekly music column for local newspaper *The Star*, in which he mentioned 1960s band The Byrds as often as he could. Colbert was also running a record store in Dunedin. Records Records was named after a shop in Los Angeles called Records Records Records, run by a cocaine-snorting, soap-opera-watching guy who sold albums to the city's rock critics. Inspired by this example, Colbert told me that he and his girlfriend never opened the shop unless they were stoned, and in its earliest years, stocked it with bongs and hash pipes, rolling papers and colourful posters. Colbert sold albums he was given to review, damaged vinyl from the major labels, as well as taking second-hand albums to sell on commission. As Dunedin's music scene had become a fulcrum for original songs and lively gigs, Records Records was a centre for everyone in town whose lives were caught up in listening to and making music.

It is worth noticing this history for a few reasons, not least because of the way the psychedelic music of the 1960s confused the usual focus upon the songwriter. Amidst the reverberation of multiple guitarists and vocalists, the singer and song no longer channel the energy of a band, that is instead diffused through fractured riffs and extended, free-form freakouts on stage. Psychedelic music put the songwriter on notice for dominating the band, for putting instruments in their place, making them subservient to the song rather than letting them loose to express themselves. While The Byrds and The Grateful Dead brought psychedelic sounds to the North American masses, the equality of players implicit in psychedelic music found its improvisational apogee in Europe in such Krautrock collectives as Amon Düül and Kluster, as well as Faust, Neu and Popol Vuh, whose hippie lives coincided with albums of freeform, transcendent guitarism and electronica. Their experimentation is as much a precedent for The Dead C as the floating pop that came out of Dunedin in the 1980s as, like The Dead C, Krautrock acts created a discipline around the freedom to play together in ways that developed distinct syntheses of pulsating rock.

Rock music was not so visionary by the 1990s. While The Byrds' 'Turn Turn Turn' (1965) became a soundtrack for protests against the Vietnam War, and the best of Krautrock came out of experimental living communes, in the 1990s the terms of rebellion had become a part of the double-speak of late capitalist life. Mobilizsing political protest became more difficult as the terms of revolution had become a part of popular culture. Speaking out on civil rights and war had, by the 1990s, given way to an ambivalence around politics in popular and underground culture.

The ambivalent forms of The Dead C's records are a long way from a 1990s generation of grunge and shoegaze music, but they do echo the way that musicians of this moment stepped back from the big picture, and no longer sought to use songs to carry messages about peace, social justice, or the environment. Authenticity was instead to be found in fuzzy guitars. The Dead C are part of this historical return to guitars, drums, and distortion, but rather than blur it all together as grunge and shoegaze did, it is possible to hear individual instruments at work in their sound. It's a classical guitar sound rather than one that blurs into other guitars, and one that sits alongside the total electrical system that Russell in particular is playing, as he fiddles the knobs and plugs of his amplifier, dragging and shaking the guitar in front of it to make a screeching blast of combined distortion and feedback. Carter remembers when The Dead C supported Sonic Youth in Christchurch in 1993, that 'for some of the set he didn't even plug in his guitar. He just made noises with the end of his lead, sticking it into the wood of the stage'.[6]

While The Dead C's sound is always more than the sum of its parts, the types of noises Morley, Russell and Yeats are typically making can be heard apart from each other on their records, not because they are in a multitrack studio, but because the sounds themselves are so distinct. Most of the time anyway. This allows the ear to shift from guitar to drum to vocal, from one kind of distortion to the next; it is this movement that creates the totality of The Dead C's sound rather than a fuzzy or thrashy blur. The band is a kind of triptych, a portrait of each member as much as a mashing together of them.

By this second side of *Clyma* things are all that much louder and more indistinct. 'Power' takes more of a story form than 'Sky', telling the U.S. to take their 'shit out of here':

Tentative power
relax Panama

hell has come now
hell has come
my baby was shot
my house was bombed
I've got no food
there is no water
my teeth need attention
my back is sore
they shut down the water
they've stolen our teacher
all we want is for you to be out of here
and a life from fear
take your fucking shit out of here
take your fucking shit out …

Something follows here that I cannot make out on any of the versions of 'Power', since by now everyone in the band is preoccupied with making a racket. Perhaps it is not important, since on the 1991 seven-inch of the track (*Mighty/Power/Peace*) the vocals finish on 'take your fucking shit out', as the band keeps to a slower version of the beat to fade down into the clunky aftermath of a thin vinyl pressing.

The larger historical picture informs Morley's lyrics. While the US invasion of Panama in 1989 and 1990 is its subject, its 1990 release was framed by a media picture from Palestine and the noise of the track can be interpreted as a frustrated answer to the ongoing military invasions and occupations of countries around the world. The noisiness of the track speaks to the ambivalence of making art or releasing records when the world is going to shit. The historic, televisual and personal, are suspended alongside each other as Morley sings to 'you' and 'they', telling the US to get out of Panama but also to get out of his head, to fuck off so that he can live without fear, to get on with 'important things'.

The lyrics sharpen The Dead C's rambling, sonic intensity, their driving, crushing inferno of rock instruments repurposed for precise ends. Morley uses the noise to focus his lyrical sensibility, to charm The Dead C in a certain direction, as he shifts from negative image to negative image, from renting his arse to those dumb fucks, and from a bombed-out house to having a sore back and teeth. In Power 'they' are the US, who shot his baby and bombed his house, but the warzone is also on televisions everywhere, spreading the grief, outrage and violence into even the most isolated corners of the world. 'Power' anticipates the greater scale of US devastation that will come in 1991 with the Gulf War saturating screens with its bomb cams and burning oil fields.

This is the anagogical way of thinking about Morley's lyrics, but there's a more autonomous one, too, in which Morley is in retreat from this fucked up world. In this his lyrics recall a history of literary outsiders, from Herman Melville's *Bartleby* (1856) who refuses to move from the office window to Samuel Beckett's *Murphy* (1938) who ties himself to a rocking chair and Beckett's *Molloy* (1951) who lies beneath a tree sucking stones. Their characters only come to life by negating everything around them, coming into being by refusing everything that comes their way. Or fast forward to the time of *Clyma*, to the novels of Glasgow writer James Kelman whose heroes can barely express themselves through black rages and drunken blackouts, but do so anyway with a plethora of fucks, fuckts and fuck alls. Morley's alienation complements The Dead C's loose, shambling and dissonant version of rock. Amidst an apocalyptic clamour, he creates a poetics of wilful solitude.

After the well-practiced 'Power', the track 'Highway' plays out the idea that the band should do a quick thrash song at every gig. Lax writes that it 'most aptly exemplifies the description of the Dead C's sound as "a garbage truck backing over the abyss".'[7] Morley shouts over Russell's and Yeats's playing as fast as they can before the track (or truck) stops suddenly and uncannily, as if they had planned this synchronicity all along. 'Ein Kampf, Ein Seig' follows, a fast metal number that, like 'Highway', does not last past a minute. Lax says the song is 'like a goddamn blitzkrieg' as it takes the piss out of the thrash metal that had become a mainstream phenomenon at this time.[8]

It is with a sigh of relief that *Clyma* settles back into the rock atmospherics we became used to on the first side of the album, with the sensationally good 'World'. Slowly building from a guitar riff and the tapping of cymbals, 'World' becomes a mighty ballad. Morley sings over steady drums as Russell's guitar noodles in and out of a riff before the song culminates in a chamber of heightened, trebly and warbled lines of flight that extend for a good couple of minutes. Yeats, typically the one to disrupt synchrony by switching rhythms, here maintains a steady, seductive swirl of pace that leads much of the recording. As with 'Electric', this coming together will conclude with a slow guitar that carries on the central riff of 'World', breathing into the quiet as a lingering echo of the sonic avalanche that had come before. A cheer and a few claps end the track, presumably from Lax in the corner.

'World' is as conventional as The Dead C get, which is to say not very, and proves their mettle as composers, showing that songs could be written, rehearsed and performed if only this is what the band wanted to do. Here it is difficult to make out what Morley is singing about, his voice elucidating the band's atmosphere, his low and often mournful tone smoothing over any jagged angles the other two might make. Morley's mournful poetics pull the melody out from the disassembled rock instrumentation that makes up 'World', turning a spinning riff from something that sounds interesting into one of The Dead C's most enigmatic compositions. It's a beautiful song, and one that appears in another version on a 1994 compilation, *World Peace Hope Et Al (1988–1993)*, which assembles various recordings from the early Dead C years. This latter version was recorded in front of an actual crowd, who banter with Russell, and spur the band on to a more intense, shattering final section. The two versions prove The Dead C's capacity as songwriters, as this track has everything in it to make an epic, dare I say post-rock, classic and it is something that they had evidently played before, as it hangs together in a well-practiced arrangement. Here and on *World Peace Hope Et Al* it remains an obscure number, buried in the mixes of both albums.

4 An Englishman Does Not Share the Droll Humour of the Local People

The cover of *Clyma* is a tribute-cum-pisstake of The Fall's live 1981 album *Totale's Turns*. The idea of making it lies somewhere amidst Lax's final days in New Zealand. In 'Cowbell' he is a surprisingly succinct guide to the flippant maze of references that populate *Clyma*'s cover, from baseball players to local drinking establishments, somehow recalled from a blurry weekend a foggy few decades ago.[1] Morley scribbled and typeset the front cover and Lax wrote the notes on the back, in a stoner agreement that this was going to be a pretty good stunt to pull. *Totale's Turns* is less well known than The Fall's classic *Hex Enduction Hour* of 1982, that was praised for its anti-cover, a bunch of scribbled notes hardly lending themselves to the eye of anyone rifling through the record bin for something flashy. *Totale's Turns* is not much more compelling to the eye, made up mostly a plain white sleeve with THE FALL printed on the top right-hand corner, and a handwritten list of touring locations below. It's like a box someone has scribbled onto so that they know what's on the inside, rather than an advertisement or even a concept of the band and its sound.

Totale's Turns cannot be understood without grasping the consciousness of northern English people of being different from those in the south and the anti-commercialism of The Fall's songwriter Mark E Smith. The working-class towns listed on the back of *Totale's Turns* are not virtue signalling, as we might say today, but a critique of the way English bands from the north want to escape their roots and become a part of London's high and cosmopolitan life. Rather than Berlin or New York, Smith lists their tour of obscure working men's clubs in Northern England, writing 'Doncaster! Bradford! Preston! Prestwich!' on the cover. The working class, northern identity of this part of England is echoed by the cynicism the Christchurch and Dunedin music underground developed about Auckland on the North Island of New Zealand. *Totale's Turns* and *Clyma* represent a struggle from the periphery of their respective countries, albums that wanted to do something different that was neither populist nor too self-indulgent.

The *Clyma* cover drops faux-tour and faux-place names: 'Harrington, Greystoke, Curriemeade, Koputai!' Here they even pulled the wool over Lax's eyes. He writes in 'Cowbell' that these are places on the Otago Peninsula, across the water from Port Chalmers. Greystoke is Tarzan's true name and a country estate in England, while there is no Harrington or Curriemeade. Koputai, however, is the Maori name for Port Chalmers, so it's true to Russell's house where *Clyma* was recorded. Below this Te Wai Pounamu is the Maori name for the South Island, offering some truth amidst all this fiction.

Mark E Smith was something of a hero in New Zealand not only for the distinct, charismatic music of The Fall, but also because he was so stubbornly independent. He was renowned for endlessly writing music and doing it so quickly that much of it was never recorded. He would change band line-ups and the rules of the game for the band members, to sabotage both their expectations and that of his fans. Russell remembers that

Maryrose Crook, who helped with their tour of New Zealand, told him it was,

> like Mark E. Smith and a rugby league team. That's how it worked. Basically there's a bunch of boys who want to drink beer and talk about football. And Mark E Smith was running the show, he clicked his fingers and they did stuff.[2]

For those who played with him, Smith was a despotic prankster who pissed off everyone he encountered, but he also had some seriously sophisticated ideas about what it meant to be an anarchist poet alive at the cusp of neo-liberal state capture.

The Fall, as English cultural critic Mark Fisher writes, mash together the working class and the avant-garde, the popular and the difficult, to elude the traps of both commodification and art-wank at the same time.[3] In his lyrics, and in the occasional missive, Smith speaks through the character of Totale, from whom the title of *Totale's Turns* comes. Totale is a ludicrously dressed, tentacled entertainer on the working men's club circuit, and Fisher suggests a figure for the return of the north of England to its nineteenth-century glory. Totale's time has, however, passed, as England has careened into mass unemployment and union busting, the collapse of industrial labour and the birth of a post-industrial yuppie society.

Turn *Totale's Turns* over and on the back sleeve is a typewritten statement signed R. Totale XVIII, in which he hopes that 'one day a Northern sound will emerge not tied to that death-circuit attitude or merely reiterating movements based in the capital' of London. The statement is, in turn, reproduced with variations on the back of *Clyma. T.* As Totale XXVIIII, Lax writes that:

<u>YOU CALL YOURSELVES BLOODY PROFESSIONALS</u>?

was one of the shower-cum-dressing room comments the Dead C received after completing their 'turn' which makes up both sides of this record, along with 'Everybody knows the best groups cum frmt Auckland' and 'You'll never work again'. Many people have commented on the Non Working Mens Club aspect of the Dead C's work, usually people who've had to live with or treat W.M.C.'s as the only form of live entertainment. Anyway, satire always takes a while to get through, and that N.W.M.C. mentality is alive and well except nowadays it wears straight-leg Levi's. Maybe one day a Southern sound will emerge not tied to that Flying Nun pop-circuit attitude or merely reinterating movements based in the north.

Enough, both sides were recorded in front of a 100% home-brew sodden audience, and we <u>always</u> feel like preaching, to the converted especially.

I don't particularly like any of the persons on this L.P. That said, I marvel at their guts. This is probably the most inaccurate document of the Dead C ever released, even though they'll have a hard time convincing their mums and dads about that, ha ha.

– T. Totale XXVIIII
Honorary Member,
Careys Bay Young Drinkers Club

There is a droll sort of humour at play in both texts from Manchester and Dunedin, written some ten years apart, that are typical of first the fast-talking, thieving culture of working-class Manchester and of Lax imitating the sardonic mood of Dunnerites on a good day.

The irony of the argument that a 'Northern Sound will emerge' and that 'a Southern sound will emerge not tied to that Flying Nun pop-circuit attitude or merely reiterating movements based in the north', is that both The Fall and The Dead C did anticipate a new sound from their own geographies. Although Smith came to loathe the post-punk synthesis that came out of Manchester's Factory records, the rhetoric around it was all about finding a new popular music for the smart working classes. Smith fantasized about playing into the collapse of Britain over the course of the twentieth century, and Factory's saccharine synth-pop was salving the wounds with cheese and biscuits. The Dead C also thought of themselves as making albums in the aftermath, as Flying Nun had, by the 1990s, become a spectre of the past hanging over Dunedin, representing a nostalgia that the Dead C wanted to overcome with a new way of doing things.

The differences of geography and terminology on the cover of *Clyma* are not quite parody as 'straight-leg Lee Coopers' becomes 'straight-leg Levi's', 'an 80% disco weekend mating audience' becomes 'a 100% home-brew sodden audience', and the 'Working Men's Club aspect of The Fall's work' is on *Clyma* the 'Non-Working Mens Club aspect of The Dead C's work'. Rather than a mealy-mouthed band from working-class Manchester, The Dead C come from a culture in which work has lost its place as the fount of cultural and social identity. After the boom-and-bust capitalism of the 1980s, the romanticism of the working class has long been succeeded by a deep mistrust of society at large. As Morley intones, work is just renting your arse, and you don't mean much anyway.

The Fall also have a very particular history in New Zealand, holding a troubled place in the Flying Nun story. When they toured the country in 1982, Chris Knox thought he had made a verbal deal to record and release one of their New Zealand gigs. Knox was the charismatic punk who had inspired Dunedin

An Englishman Does Not Share

with his antics in The Enemy in the late 1970s, and who had recorded the *Dunedin Double* EP (1982) on his four track, putting the town on the world's musical map. Nobody was going to argue with Knox, even with the cheesy cover he made for the *Fall in a Hole* (1983) double LP of the Auckland show. It featured a photograph of smiling bass player Marc Riley arriving at the airport in Christchurch, alongside a Knox cartoon.[4]

The cover would prove out of time with The Fall as, by the time they left Sydney on their tour of the antipodes, Riley was no longer in the band. He'd had an exchange of blows with Smith. This was one reason why Smith was so pissed off when he saw the record on sale as an expensive import in England. Knox later admitted that he had not sent Smith a test pressing and had not had any contact with The Fall since a late-night, beer-soaked conversation in Knox's Auckland lounge room. The only hole that anyone would be falling into was one that Flying Nun had dug for itself, as it attempted to shift its costly boxes of thousands of LPs without drawing too much attention to itself.

If there's something that both The Fall, or at least Mark E Smith, and The Dead C have in common, it's their avant-gardism and independence. Smith released a small mountain of material on independent labels and sabotaged any opportunity he had of making The Fall commercially successful.[5] He also took complete control of The Fall's albums in the studio, deleting instruments while overdubbing others. Russell has said that this kind of post-production influenced the way The Dead C mixed their albums; it can be heard here and there on *Harsh 70s Reality*, but *Clyma* breaks with this kind of finessing.

Let's not, however, read the *Clyma* cover as being completely indebted to The Fall, or to their infamous misunderstanding with Flying Nun. While The Fall were one of a small handful of well-known bands from the awful 1980s that were respected by The Dead C and Lax alike, *Clyma*'s parody-cum-tribute is not to be taken too seriously, its flippancy a part of the whole package of a record that is both a dedicated document of a serious jam and a weekender whim. It's less about The Fall than about the vinylophilic sensibility of the record collector, a game played between Lax and the band who had a boundless enthusiasm for interesting music. This was how Siltbreeze began, with Lax's dogged interest in getting albums released that he would like to own, but that weren't out yet, and that nobody else wanted to manufacture.[6]

Lax and The Dead C had the record collecting game in mind when they decided to first press *Clyma* as a bootleg, pressing the first 300 copies under the drunken name of Proletariat Idiots Productshun (Zzzz …) scribbled on the back cover. The joke would become serious when Lax returned to find The Dead C had become something of an interest among North American collectors of the subaltern:

> After a day of re-acclimating myself (culture shock) another mind bender presented itself: Harsh 70's was practically out of print. Even the last of the Helen/Bury LPs had become spoken for. What the fuck? Great news, for sure. With a couple of well-timed checks rolling in, I was able to get *Clyma* off to Hub Serval (a now-defunct record pressing plant where the majority of early Siltbreeze released were manufactured) post haste. By mid-June it was ready. I spent a morning on my sidewalk, spray-mounting the front and back covers, wearing a charcoal-filtered breathing mask (so as not to inhale fumes and airborne glue). Fun? Oh, yes, the likes of which you cannot imagine. Eight weeks prior, the original pressing (on

Proletariat Idiot) of 350 copies seemed like a reasonable number. Now? Well, let's see.

The thing sold out in a day. Customers were downright ANGRY that they couldn't get copies. 'You have FUCKED me,' one letter read. And while it sucked to be him, I wasn't so keen to don mask and glue up a bunch more record jackets. After a quick (expensive) call down to PC, it was decided to hell with the bootleg design, let's just do it as a legit Siltbreeze release (SB-16), 1,000 of which were made. This time the buying and selling was not so fanatical. It went out of print, eventually; by about 1996, it wasn't so easy to come by.[7]

The new editions had Siltbreeze and Xpressway neatly printed where Proletariat Idiots had once been, claiming the record back from total silliness and potential obscurity.

The mishmash of references on the cover, from The Fall to Gong's *Gong Est Mort, Vive Gong* (1977) are as relevant to the album as is The Fall's *Totale's Turns*, which is to say not very. They are instead part of the obsessive gathering of collections of records, information and useless facts required for psychically navigating a culturally isolated, pre-internet New Zealand. The references would, of necessity, be insider ones. Who else is to know that Harrington, Greystoke and Curriemeade are not towns in the south of the country, or that Clyma was the name of Morley's recently deceased cat? He was 'the gnarliest cat that I have ever known', he told me as recently as 2019, but Russell insists that the title is 'an ironic tribute, because no one in the world actually liked the disgusting creature. Everyone complains about their pets, but I have to say it, Michael, Clyma was one of the worst'. You'll also notice the alliteration between *Clyma Est Mort* and *The Dead C*, that comes to resemble the Dead Clyma or the Dead Cat.

The Dead C were playing this intertextual game from their very first cassette release. Morley sings the poetry of Max Harris on *Dead See Perform M Harris* (1987). Harris was the founder of Angry Penguins, an Australian literary magazine best known for being hoaxed by a couple of conservatives pretending to be a modernist poet. Nobody in Australia liked experimental modernist art and poetry in the 1940s, but the irony is that the fake poems turned out to be pretty good and are now some of the most celebrated antipodean poetry. The Dead C also declare that they are pretending to make rock music, Russell in particular claiming no ability on his own part, yet they make great rock music, pretending to be the band that they become, hoaxing themselves as much as the rest of the world in the process. Singing false poetry is somehow appropriate, then, as The Dead C pretend to be something they really are.

The ironic precedent for The Dead C in Dunedin's small world of music is The Stones, one of the best live acts playing the town in the 1980s. Bass player Jeff Batts declared that The Stones wanted to do 'everything the wrong way', including sharing a band name with The Rolling Stones.[8] He would tell crowds how great The Stones were, and that 'We want to be God'. They collaged their skinny bodies onto a mock-up of The Rolling Stones's *Exile on Main St* (1972) for the *Dunedin Double* cover, and sung some of the silliest lyrics over great rock riffs to parody the drive for fame and success. Again, the relationship of the South Island to a big band from overseas is an ambiguous one as, after touring there, Keith Richards from The Rolling Stones called the town of Invercargill to the south of Dunedin the 'arsehole of the world'.[9] In his recent biography Richards is probably confusing Dunedin with Invercargill when he writes of Dunedin in the 1960s as a 'black hole … I don't think you could find anything more depressing anywhere. Dunedin made Aberdeen seem like Las Vegas'. Many living in Dunedin or Invercargill might agree with him, but for the fact that the slur comes from one of the most successful musicians in the world.

The irony is that in parodying the Rolling Stones, Dunedin's The Stones could play as well as anyone else, and that in taking the piss out of rock they become the very thing that they were parodying. Morley remembers The Stones were the best band to see in Dunedin at the time, with superb combinations of riffs and drums cycling around each other. 'They were Neanderthal', writes Matthew Bannister of pop band Sneaky Feelings, understating the way in which they were cleverly taking the piss out of the ambitions of serious bands like his own.[10] Russell remembers seeing them support The Clean at a university orientation gig in the early 1980s, playing with the projected movies *Altered States* (1980) and *Flash Gordon* (1980). Rather than being a part of the serious competition between Dunedin songwriters, The Stones were having fun, with a dry and self-deprecating humour that The Dead C would bring to *Clyma*.

5 The Natural Born Gifts of the Drummer

While The Stones are one Dunedin predecessor, The Clean are another, in the sense that they were the example for all the Dunedin acts who followed. Even The Stones, joking around in every interview they did, admitted that The Clean were the best band in the world, and that 'Our ambition is to have them support us'.[1] Yeats saw them when he was fifteen, 'playing in their socks'.[2] Russell paid a dollar and fifty cents to see them in November 1981 at the Empire Tavern, realizing, along with many others in the crowd, that this was the best band you could imagine. The epiphany did not go away even after Russell had moved to London in 1986, where he saw nothing as good as most Dunedin acts he'd been seeing before he left.

The November 1981 gig also featured The Verlaines, who were trying out songs that Graeme Downes had written but that the band could barely play, in something of a recurring story for the Dunedin acts of the time. The earliest Clean gigs showed 'a lack of musical ability and elegance', and simply 'bad playing'.[3] And yet such improficiency made Dunedin a compelling place to see live music, as audiences witnessed bands developing material from gig to gig. Dunedin's music critic Roy Colbert remembered 'false starts forgotten words, unintentional key changes, ignored cues, the lot'.[4] 'Shambolic' is the word most used to describe The Clean's early live qualities, their reverberating wall of guitar noise putting some people off while captivating others.

There was an equality to this kind of playing on stage before you could actually play an instrument. The Clean's drummer Hamish Kilgour sees his band living out the legacy of punk, keeping musicality out of the music because '[t]he person standing watching us play is no better or different than I am, and we want to keep it that way. I hate drum rostroms because it's like elevating yourself above people'.[5] They would start and stop in the middle of songs, while songwriter and Hamish's brother David Kilgour would ask Hamish or bass player Robert Scott to change this or that. In Dunedin, songs were written and tried out on a crowd that night, rather than cleaned up and rehearsed to infinity. Rather than bopping out at the front of the stage, their dedicated audience would often sit on the floor wearing their winter scarves, stoned and intent on listening to the shifts in beat and melody that the band were striving for.

This was the brilliance of The Clean – that beneath Hamish's loose drumming, David's reverberating guitar and Robert Scott's bass echoing through it all, in this rollicking, somehow cohering mash of beautiful sound, lie songs of pointed sophistication. Take the B-side of their first single for Flying Nun, the song 'Platypus' on *Tally Ho!/Platypus* (1981), which after beginning with a slow, easy rhythm, suddenly speeds into an anxious rock riff with a piercing, biting guitar. Over the change David is asking, 'Do you want to go, do you want to go, do you want to go?' harassing us into making a decision we cannot make. These swings of mood and tone characterize The Clean's most compelling tracks. After 'Platypus' a small crowd give a dull clap, a nodding rather than roaring approval, opening a tiny aural window onto New Zealand in 1981. The tracks are short and sharp, their fuzzy combination of instruments, and the occasional syncopation, pointing to a sophisticated sense of how songs work to make a mood, to build an idea.

The way in which these rough and ready recordings fall away from their own perfection makes for a friendly aesthetic that allows one's ears in, inviting us to join the band's meditation on shared concerns about 'Getting Older', 'What You Should Be Now', 'What You're Thinkin' Now' or 'The End of My Dream'. The Clean were not to last, however, with David feeling the pressure of ever-rotating gigs, and would break up in 1982 after just a handful of years, and at the height of their powers. By the time Lax had heard them in North America, they had already broken up. 'Mind boggling!' he writes (they did reform in 1988).[6] While other Flying Nun bands went on to be seduced by big labels and big studios, these early recordings by The Clean retain a sense of immediacy that captures something of the small, energetic, and unpolished world of Dunedin in the early 1980s.

While many who saw The Clean at this time remember their stops and starts, their inability to play, Verlaines songwriter Graeme Downes was inspired by the complexity of their compositions. He was classically trained and prided himself on making complex and hard-to-play songs, adding in instruments that are uncommon on pop and rock albums including the clarinet and oboe. Downes has been the most vocal about the role of songwriting in driving the Flying Nun bands, and The Clean were the masters. He writes that 'sociological factors and a description of their peculiar sound' do not explain their influence, instead arguing for their compositional brilliance.[7] In treating 'Point that Thing Somewhere Else' like a Bach concerto, he wants to sideline the kind of looseness that The Clean brought to their playing, the way that songs speed up and slow down, the shambolic quality that they brought to recording. He also neglects the way that early Dunedin Sound bands, including his own, were recorded almost in the process of composing their songs, making for a jangly aesthetic. Musicians reach for notes while falling short of them, playing out a sense that life is not what one expected it to be.

Inspired by The Clean, a teenage Yeats auditioned to play in Downes's band,

> I lied my way into The Verlaines, told them I could play drums. I remember overhearing them talking about me, like, oh, he can't keep time but he's got some dynamic. I was at one side of the room and they were all huddled together on the other, talking about me. At once point I heard someone say, 'he can't even fucking count to six'.[8]

It's the kind of memory that comes to mind after a few decades playing in The Dead C, and echoes Russell's insistence that they were amateurs striving to get better as amateurs.

Bassist Jane Dodd remembers Yeats's tryout differently, however. She had been with Martin Phillipps's teenage band The Same before The Verlaines, playing a high school prom and a talent quest, as well as with Phillipps's The Chills for a few months. By this stage, Dodd knew what it took to play an instrument. She remembers that they:

> auditioned several drummers for The Verlaines. Robbie stood head and shoulders above everyone else. There's unusual time signatures in The Verlaines, and Robbie was the only one who could make a good fist of working with the changes and crazy rhythms. He blew us away, he can think very laterally and be loose, he's very unstructured in his thoughts about rhythms and songs.

Dodd makes the point that although The Verlaines and The Dead C appear a galaxy apart from each other, they share Yeats's talent for unconventional drumming. His ability to turn a song around with a few throws of the sticks brings a different sensibility to a performance. While Downes and Russell are full of opposing ideas about what's good in a performance, Yeats is there in both of their bands, pushing the conventions of the song in different ways, to places that they do not typically go. Downes does this with difficult compositions, while Russell plays his amplifier, and Yeats's virtuoso drumming is the constant between them.

The first record The Verlaines released with Yeats on drums was the *10 O'Clock in the Afternoon* EP in 1984, the photograph on its back cover betraying something of the unspoken truth of many bands run by a songwriter. Downes stands over Dodd and Yeats who sit on a park bench. It is meant to be a relaxed, English sort of a scene, but Downes also holds a stick in one hand and it is difficult not to see it as a metaphor for the composer holding sway over his players.

A very young, red-haired Yeats can also be seen crouched over his drums on the video for the album's 'Pyromaniac'. There's not an ease to his playing here, as all three members of the band are focused intently on their instruments, and it is likely that they have only just learned the song, Downes included. *10 O'Clock in the Afternoon* is the least complex of Verlaines releases, the easiest to listen to and the most consistent as it shifts from song to song. Made in the wake of the successful *Dunedin Double* and the 'Death and the Maiden' single, Downes remembers that it was 'creativity on the fly, no pre-production, no demoing of songs'.[9] The EP was Flying Nun's format for bands not quite ready to put out a full LP, and you can hear the energy of the band following up their recent successes.

Andrew Schmidt describes Yeats's 'awkward, apt beat' for The Verlaines and there is a sense of youthful intensity about the records he played on through the 1980s.[10] As Yeats recalls, 'The Verlaines had already made the *Dunedin Double* record when I joined them, and I was like, fuck, I might get to play drums on a record!'[11] He may have brought to the Verlaines more than Downes might have bargained for. Music critic Gary Steel remembers seeing The Verlaines in the winter of 1985, a performance marred by a drummer so drunk he could not keep time.[12] In Steel's eyes, Yeats was symptomatic of the whole scene in which some decent songwriting was obscured by the 'meaningless and boring jangle' of off-tune guitars.[13]

It may be that in the quest for great songs, the songwriters of Dunedin did not concern themselves as much about the technicalities of performance. As Russell points out, Downes

Figure 3 *Yeats on drums at Grey Street during the* Clyma *sessions. Photo Tom Lax.*

used amplifiers that were not his own when he was on tour, plugging his guitar into whatever he had borrowed, hearing the note he was playing rather than the sound. Russell, on the other hand, cares less about the overall vision of a song or improvised session than he does on how it is sounding through his 1961 Concord Contessa. The Concord and other broken amplifiers have been much more important to Russell than his guitars, having enabled him to develop unique sounds through the distortion they are wired for. Russell can be said to play the amplifier rather than the guitar, as he moves about on stage in relation to the amplifier, wavering and wobbling the circuit of feedback with his body, microphone and guitar strings.

It may be that Yeats was drunk in his performance with The Verlaines, but his drumming out of time was part of an historical pattern being worked out in Dunedin, in which musicianship is not as important as other aspects of a performance, such as the song (Downes) or the sound (Russell). By the time of *Clyma* Yeats has some tricks up his sleeve. He plays to anarchic type on 'Sunshine-Dirt for Harry', breaking up any certainties we may have about where this track is going. In The Dead C, Yeats could play without someone telling him how to play. Rather than making music to a score, he was blaring improvised rock, dissolving songs on a whim only to begin again and start another. He keeps the time on 'World', however, playing behind the beat for the slow, melodic parts while playing ahead of the beat in its final, instrumental section. It's a tour de force as, after listening to an unpredictable and uneven album, suddenly Yeats offers us something sublime.

Yeats is a bridge between the Dunedin bands of the 1980s and the Port Chalmers's free noise of the 1990s, drumming amidst the songwriting culture of the 1980s before pushing the rock song to a jammy, chaotic place with The Dead C.

Amidst Morley's downstepping riffs and the squeal of Russell's amplifier he holds the band to a rock aesthetic. David Eggleton writes that the band made 'what some would hear as chaotic, screeching feedback held together by the organic drumming of Robbie Yeats' and it's true that as the other sounds on The Dead C's recordings twist beyond recognition, the drums offer a way of anchoring the blare.[14] Playing out the two sides of the Dunedin scene, Yeats shifts from the tight-arsed complexity of Downes's songwriting to the shambolic, low-cost Dead C. At around the same time, Yeats was making his last record with The Verlaines, *Some Disenchanted Evening* (1990), he was also drumming for what would become The Dead C's *Eusa Kills*. The Verlaines were recording in an Auckland studio, with a budget to match, while The Dead C were in Dunedin living rooms and using The Verlaine's porta-studio.

If there is a precedent to Yeats's craft amidst the small world of Dunedin musicians, it's in Hamish Kilgour's just-off-the-rhythm drumming for The Clean. Hamish is a stoned virtuoso on tracks like 'Platypus' and 'At the Bottom' that slow down and speed up with the dynamics of the song. He pulls in and out of the beat, chiming into and out of the guitar parts, turning the drums into an expression of his loose personality. Yeats takes the free-wheeling charm of Hamish's shifting tempos to a stubborn extreme, sometimes hammering the cymbals while leaving the rest of the kit alone, whileat others thundering through a quiet patch with a marching rhythm that comes through the guitars like a parade.

6   On the Poetics of the Bible, and the Day Jobs of the Artists

Dunedin's isolation and its gloomy weather has given rise to a long-running conversation around the geography of Dunedin, and its place in fostering a closely knit culture of music making. Many of the musicians who were part of Flying Nun's success barely travelled elsewhere until opportunities to tour overseas came in the mid-to-late 1980s. Money was hard to come by. Most were on the dole or working in dead-end jobs, and sometimes on 'work for the dole' programmes for Flying Nun.

When Sonic Youth toured New Zealand in 1993 and asked The Dead C to support them, Morley was almost thirty and hadn't yet left the country. The connection had been made years before, after Morley drove them around Auckland when they played there in 1989, pissing off the promoters who didn't know where their rock stars had gone. He'd also given them a copy of *The Sun Stabbed EP* (1988), that Russell had released on Xpressway, introducing them to both The Dead C and the then new label. With gigs ahead of them in Australia and Japan it is possible that Sonic Youth never listened to *Sun Stabbed*, but by the time they returned to New Zealand in 1993 they were well aware of both. At each of their New Zealand gigs they finished with 'Expressway to Yr Skull', the 1986 Sonic Youth track that Russell had named Xpressway after. On this second Sonic Youth tour The Dead C would also piss off the promoters who had to fly them around the country and put them up in hotels, and lost an opportunity to sell the support slot to an ambitious newer band. The Sonic Youth audience were 'nonplussed and bemused'. As one punter described it, The Dead C were 'either really bad, or they're just joking'.[1]

When Morley first left New Zealand in 1994 it was with Gate rather than The Dead C. He toured with members of Sonic Youth to play the north-east coast (*Live in Boston, NYC 1994* documents the Boston gig with Lee Renaldo, and the New York gig with electric harp player Zeena Parkins) and went on to briefly become a part of the reinvented Krautrock band Faust in San Francisco (see Faust's *Rein* album of 1995). This adventure was something of a dream come true for Morley, who had only come to know music through records, and not at live gigs. Imagine never leaving New Zealand, only to go overseas to play alongside Sonic Youth, Faust and Keiji Haino!

While it is impossible to get reliable statistics on the fact, it is thought that New Zealanders were the biggest buyers of vinyl in the world during the 1970s and 1980s. Morley played a big part in this collective mania for records, amassing an impressive number from the time he was a teenager. In 1980 and 1981, Morley was packing bags in a supermarket in the suburbs of Napier on the North Island. He was one of thousands of young people tuning into Barry Jenkin's radio show as it came in and out of phase from Auckland. Russell was tuning in from Nelson, too, as the ionosphere lowered and allowed the radio waves through.

Jenkin was at odds with his producers as he introduced the country to punk and new wave, with schoolkids recording his radio shows onto cassette and passing them between themselves. They were also ordering records that they'd read about in the British *NME* and *Zig Zag* magazines. The guy in the local bookstore let Morley and his school friends read them without paying. After reading the classifieds they would write off to order releases from mail order companies in the UK, especially ska, punk and post-punk, early industrial and what would become known as indie. These addresses set the precedent for Siltbreeze and Xpressway, that along with a bunch of other home labels took the mail-order method and ran with it to create an underground exchange.

If the minor labels didn't offer shipping to New Zealand, Morley's friend Richard Ram would get records shipped to his UK-based grandparents who then sent them on. Releases on smaller labels weren't available in New Zealand, or would come a long time after they were released. Sometimes they'd pay horrendous amounts of money, paying postage from the other side of the world, for albums that they'd never heard before but that sounded interesting. Sometimes the records would arrive months later only to have been warped in transit, but this didn't discourage their vinylophilia.

Morley remembers ordering Cabaret Voltaire and The Residents, Young Marble Giants and The Go Betweens. Ram remembers getting Linton Kwesi Johnson and Joy Division in the mail. Morley also got cassettes from a penpal in London, who recorded New Order and various Peel Sessions for him. A part of this interest in connecting with the UK was to get better quality product. Ram remembers a Joy Division record coming from the UK with embossed text on the cover and a chalk insert, while the equivalent New Zealand release had none of this fancy décor.

By the time Morley moved to Dunedin he had a substantial record collection that would impress the locals. Yeats remembers that Morley and Russell were 'freaks, man those are the guys that import records. Which was a big fucking deal'.[2]

After a lonely year attempting to get interested in anthropology at Otago University in 1982, Morley convinced Ram to move to Dunedin in 1983. Back in Napier, Morley and Ram had been jamming and recording onto Ram's parent's cassette player, in what would become the Dunedin band Wreck Small Speakers on Expensive Stereos. Ram had learned classical guitar and held their songs together with intricate bass riffs, while Morley made melodies with guitar, synthesizers, and vocals. Carter remembers that 'We always got the pair mixed up, because they were both immigrants from the north who wore the same jerseys and had the same springy brown hair.'[3] The jerseys did, in fact, have the same maker. Ram's mother had knitted a blue-grey jersey for him, and Morley thought it was great, so she knitted him a green one. They were outsiders, having come from elsewhere and arriving too late to witness the earliest gigs of the Flying Nun bands. Rather than a drummer they had a Casiotone and were more excited by Eyeless in Gaza than the Velvet Underground, Morley's vocals more Alan Vega of Suicide than Roger McGuinn of The Byrds.

Wreck Small Speakers also set the precedent for The Dead C's methods, as at live gigs Morley and Ram would improvise, making up songs as they went along. Russell remembers this clearly, saying that 'They would just get up and invent an entire set of songs in front of an audience.'[4] Morley and Russell went on to share a house with Alastair Galbraith and Robert Scott of The Clean in 1984. The Empire Tavern was the most consistent venue in town, with music every weekend by whomever was organized enough to book themselves in. There was also Chippendale House, a warehouse organized by locals that featured experimental theatre and poetry readings as well as bands from around 1985 to 1987. The best money for gigs came from the university union who sponsored bands to play what was called a wet lunch on Fridays, wet with beer that is. They would pay $200 to anyone who could fill the slot, a good amount of money at the time. The population of drinking students had kept cover bands going in Dunedin through the 1970s, and in the 1980s were supporting original music.

Galbraith and Russell went on stage a few times together, foreshadowing A Handful of Dust, as did Morley and Russell when Galbraith could not get anyone to support his band The Rip when they played The Empire. Peter Gutteridge also invited Russell into a few rehearsals around this time too, bringing him some confidence with the guitar. There are some surviving recordings of this revolving circus of gigs, with people appearing and disappearing into the Dunedin milieu. They offer glimpses into Dunedin's live scene, too, with crowds murmuring away beneath Wreck Small Speakers records, while Morley murmurs indifferently into a microphone. Robert Scott released two Wreck Small Speakers on his cassette label, Every Secret Thing, in 1985. This and other local cassette labels were made out of the sheer determination of those who ran them, with Scott simply hooking up two or three tape recorders and making his own photocopied covers. Of the three Dead C members, Morley was the most promiscuous of players at this time, turning up on other recordings with Dunedin luminaries such as Shayne Carter, Wayne Elsey of The Stones, the Jefferies brothers as This Kind of Punishment, and Debbie Hinden, who would go on to play in Queen Meanie Puss.

Morley and Russell remember Wreck Small Speakers as being a band trying to do more than it was capable of. In recordings of their gigs there are touches of a youthful sincerity. Morley's voice reaches awkwardly for the higher register, and tracks can go on far too long, but there is a quality of songwriting that shines through it all, a sense of Morley's aspirations to create something compelling to listen to, as he shifts from different kinds of guitar playing to singing and back again.

It is tempting to argue that if Morley and Ram had been a couple of years older and had arrived in Dunedin slightly earlier, they would have been more central to Flying Nun's celebrated early history. Their sound, however, was very different to the label's guitar-oriented pop music. Using cheap, weird instruments to make long, winding and sometimes instrumental compositions, they were on the outer orbit of the kind of pop music culture that Dunedin was fostering. We can thank Ram for leaving town when he did, as this interest in a post-punk style instrumentalism surfaces again when Morley forms The Dead C some years later.

By the time Wreck Small Speakers got a Flying Nun release in 1987, the twelve-inch *River Falling Love*, Ram had moved to London. The EP is of exceptional interest to anyone tracing Morley's evolution from one act to another. *River Falling Love* lacks the driving rhythms that hold the two earlier Wreck Small Speakers cassette releases together, instead layering samples and synthesizer to shift moods. Rather than driving bass, *River Falling Love* uses layers of synthesizer and lead droning guitar in a search for something more than the song, in an ambience in which Morley speaks and moans rather than sings, and in which there is an ease with the letting tracks playing themselves out in spiralling, spellbinding slowness. There are a couple of ways in which the twelve-inch anticipates The Dead C. The first is that driving bass lines and drumbeats turn out to be unnecessary and even obstructive to making something sound pleasing to the ears, to create the kind of ambience that Morley and Ram had found in obscure industrial and post-punk albums in from the UK. *River Falling Love* also anticipates

The Dead C by using found instruments and sounds that are hard to identify for a listener, bringing a strange mystique to recordings of who knows what.

Morley is also a visual artist, and a productive one at that. From his earliest days as a collector, Morley was drawn to the visual, collecting records because of their covers, buying Cabaret Voltaire's *Red Mecca* (1981) for its blurry portrait of moving light. Morley's exhibitions often rely on a blurring of lines between music and art, such as the 1993 Pro Bono show, in which he scribbled 'Hey Fuck Me Bono' on each of the posters allocated to advertise *Achtung Baby* (1991) in Dunedin. Instead of being plastered around town, they were graffitied and arranged in a grid on the wall of Number 5 Gallery downtown. U2 had been more offensive than usual in 1991, having attacked the San Francisco cut-up artists Negativland for calling an EP *U2*.

The blurring of text and visual art that Morley brought into the gallery in this and other shows builds upon a history of New Zealand modernism. The most influential of the nation's painters, Colin McCahon, painted Bible quotes, Maori poems, and lists of numbers atop massive paintings of the sheer hills that characterize the country's landscape. Morley's solo act, Gate, is named after a series of paintings by McCahon, a sequence of abstract shapes, words, and blocks of colour. Morley compares The Dead C's name to 'a McCahon drawing that has "The Dead Christ" written across the top, and if you fold the drawing across where the C ends, you get "The Dead C."[5] McCahon's ambition, his rewriting of both modernist painting and the New Zealand landscape, echoes with The Dead C, as they overwhelm the rock song with voluminous, distorted totalities in Biblical proportions.

The band played their first show as The Dead Sea, suggested by Morley's then flatmate and drummer Stella Corkery after the poisonous inland ocean that lies amidst the Bible's promised land. They quickly changed their name to The Dead See and finally The Dead C, while still punning on Sea and See. The slippage from one to the other, from the deadly sea of salt to the dead seeing, gives the band name an Old Testament quality, and approximates the vastness of their sound. As with McCahon, there is a sense that they are in the process of creation, bringing into being that which eludes them, like some Biblical scribe attempting to translate the word of God. Rather than a transcendent Christian drama, The Dead C's heaven and hell are, however, not places for the saved or the damned, but rather part of a confused nowhere in which the dead have not risen but remain in the world.

While Morley was not a part of McCahon's generation, he was friends with McCahon's protégé Ralph Hotere, who was living on the hill above Port Chalmers, just above the Grey Street house where The Dead C recorded *Clyma*. Hotere liked Morley's paintings, and gave him a studio to work in. All three artists – McCahon, Hotere and Morley – share a graphic quality that makes their work look like record covers. Combining language and image, McCahon and Hotere were insistent about tying their work to the land around them, giving a conceptual weight to the spectacular landscape of the South Island. Morley's paintings are also made up of blocks of colour, shapes that resemble things in the outside world but hazily, as if we are discovering a verdant, cubist earth through a fog.

Morley's visual acuity would come to earn him a living in a way that music never could. Completing a Masters qualification in painting in 2007 in Christchurch, he qualified for his job in the Dunedin School of Art where, at the time of writing, he is still teaching. Bruce Russell also works managing research in an art school in Christchurch, having left Dunedin some years ago. These might sound like plush jobs, but Morley and Russell are not working at universities in populous cities. While Dunedin and Christchurch have exceptional histories of art and music-making, these institutions have functioned at a distance from these scenes. Their jobs involve lots of meetings (Russell) and intensive teaching (Morley). And unlike in wealthier universities, creative research is little supported, with activities like The Dead C being strictly after-hours pursuits. Yeats is the only one of The Dead C not working as a petty bourgeois. He, instead, makes a living as a painter and decorator with a skill in conserving heritage buildings. As Shepherd writes: 'The Dead C's success has been achieved on the backs of day jobs and obstinate longevity.'[6]

7 Looking the Horse in the Mouth

Given the long experience of the band members over the course of the 1980s, going to and from gigs, and experiencing something of a zeitgeist in the history of indie music, it is not surprising that it is possible to hear a certain confidence in The Dead C's earliest recordings. On *Dead See Perform M Harris* (1987), later re-released as *The Dead Sea Perform M Harris* (2010), there is a sense that these performers have something going for them, in a distinct conflation of low guitar noise and drumming that belies the fact that they have just come together. Morley and Yeats were more experienced in bands than Russell, who admits that not being able to play worried him early on. Soon, however, he realized that he could get away with not being able to play, that nobody was going to stop The Dead C in the middle of a gig to tell the band to get off the stage, because this simply wasn't done, although audiences may well have wanted to.

Watching The Dead C play long tracks made up of little more than three chords and falling in and out of synchrony with each other, presented challenges to the ears of those attuned to listening out for great songs. While nobody said it to their face, a few people were pissed off about The Dead C and would be bewildered later at their increasing success. In the Flying Nun offices in 1989, someone was heard to complain that they were getting an American release (*Helen Said This/ Bury* on Siltbreeze, 1990). 'It's just a big noise!' they grumbled.

Musicians that had been striving for Flying Nun style success were annoyed by songs, often very long songs, featuring one or two chords that were often made up on the spot.

The Dead C were, however, about the most fun thing Morley, Russell and Yeats had done, as nobody was telling anyone else what to do. This was no longer the culture of songwriting that Dunedin had fostered, but something else that had come to occupy its place, to become a kind of parasite upon its history. And yet, The Dead C would also push aspects of this history into new terrain, bringing into focus Steel's point about the 'infernal jangle that became the apparatus through which Dunedin bands obscured their lack of performative skills'.[1] What was true of The Dead C had been true of many Dunedin bands all along, at least until the mid-1980s when practice had taught them to play their instruments with a lot more experience. And yet the amateur origins of Dunedin's successes had, by the late 1980s, been obscured by the international success of bands like The Chills and Straitjacket Fits. The Dead C marked the beginning of a split between people who were listening to music because they wanted to hear good songwriting and playing, and those who came for something less defined, more experimental and which went to unexpected places.

The other aspect of the *M Harris* recordings is that the band say they are playing the same song on both sides of the record, but it is difficult to know amidst the noise whether it is the same song, as everything sounds different. From this inaugural moment The Dead C had discovered that they did not care much about the detail, whether Russell could hold a note, whether Yeats was in time, or if Morley was singing the same lyrics. It simply didn't matter, and with each other they could get away with playing slow, chunky melodies, drifting in and

CLYMA est mort

scene than Dunedin. Lax knew people who were both playing and running small labels between Minneapolis and New York and put out a Halo of Flies seven inch when Forced Exposure, who had planned the release, didn't want it because it didn't suit their novelty theme. Halo of Flies were in demand, and Lax was paid outright for it when he got the 'Richie's Dog' seven-inch to shops. It was, he says, a 'charmed entry' into the world of distribution.[1]

On the other side of the Pacific, Russell worked out the importance of correspondence in a country as far from record buyers as New Zealand. He explains it to a guy called Dave and a band called The Nixons:

> If they like something that someone has done overseas they write to them and tell them, sending them something of their own, exchanging information and ideas. 'You're sitting around on your chuffs waiting for someone to suddenly come up and say the Nixons are just the best band in the world, here's you know, a deal.' And that's just not how it happens. This networking thing, as I'm sure you know Dave, is how it works. People in America, Europe, Japan, all know each other. It's a very small game. Having a good name, a good ear, helps, and after a while people write to me out of the blue and go I really like X and Y. I've got this label and am interested in having these people work with me, here's some examples of what I've done. I listen to what they send me and ask 'what does this fit in with?' and then just fire it off to somebody else and say, have this if you want, and just kind of speak stuff around.[2]

Lax, too, was a furious correspondent. He wrote a letter to Flying Nun after buying The Dead C's *DR503* release while on a lunch break from his job at a publishing firm, getting a brief reply from Carter who was working there at the time.[3] Replying to letters was a full-time gig at Flying Nun, with people from other labels, fanzines and shops all asking for free copies. Among the paraphernalia Lax got back in the post was a flier advertising Xpressway tapes, with a handful listed, including one by The Dead C. Flying Nun were selling these tapes through their own mail order, but had not put prices on the flier. As good as they were at releasing records, Flying Nun were not very organized. In the 1980s, amidst the flush of The Clean's success, Roy Colbert remembers 100 covers of The Clean's *Boodle Boodle Boodle* (1981) arriving in the post without the records inside to sell to the punters at his Dunedin shop. This is because much of the grunt work of the label was done by a series of musicians, including Carter and Hamish Kilgour, working for them on dole schemes or for cash.

It was fortunate that The Dead C had managed to harass Flying Nun into doing a couple of full-length albums, *DR503* and *Eusa Kills* in 1988 and 1989, before they and other Dunedin acts were left to their own fate. These releases happened because Russell and Yeats were known to those working at the label. While Yeats was the promising young drummer for The Verlaines, Russell worked for Flying Nun in 1987, and harassed them enough to put the albums into the company's processes. When *DR503* was released, it was advertised as having 'Robbie Yeats of The Verlaines' playing on it, something that would have caught the attention of Flying Nun devotees in record shops in New York and London, although The Dead C's sound was completely different.

After working for Flying Nun, Russell could see how it was possible to mobilize a network of manufacturers and distributors across Europe and North America to sell records internationally. Flying Nun was never as organized as Russell in making these deals with people overseas, however, as Shepherd's broad taste in music and interest in supporting his artists coincided with a relative lack of administrative and business experience. His international arrangements were not great money makers, and the label carried on because of the goodwill of many of the musicians, who put up with late releases and payments.[4] This while Shepherd and business partner Gary Cope spent ludicrous amounts of money on colour covers and labels for headline acts. Partly this was because Shepherd had trouble saying no to bands, especially those with the promise of selling well, even to the extent that they could choose their own catalogue number (Tall Dwarfs' 1982 EP *Louis Likes His Daily Dip* has the irreverent Chris Knox number WEE01). The divide between bands that Flying Nun thought had commercial promise and those without set up a double-tiered system, with saleable bands getting studio expenses and colour covers, and others going without. Russell witnessed this while working at Flying Nun and set up Xpressway as a cassette label to avoid the problems of a label trying to manage its expenses while supporting artists. The cassette was an easy and accessible remedy for people wanting to send and hear music around the world.

By the end of the 1980s Xpressway was getting a lot of attention. When Carter was in New Jersey he saw Xpressway releases, rather than his own Straitjacket Fits albums, in shop windows.[5] Xpressway and Siltbreeze were part of an increasingly strong network of small, home-run labels, including Ajax, Drag City, Feel Good All Over, Hell's Half Halo, Emperor Jones, Twisted Village and the emerging behemoth mail order company Forced Exposure. These were do-it-yourself projects, run by a generation of enthusiasts working

Figure 4 *Russell in a favourite orange jumper, looking like he is doing overdubs during the* Clyma *sessions when no overdubs are audible on the recording, and Russell does not remember doing them. Photo Tom Lax.*

from their bedrooms and garages for little or no money, but with an appetite for interesting and independent sound. They recognized that there would be a handful of people in each place that were enthusiastic about the kind of music they were enthusiastic about, and that these people would be enthusiastic enough to order it by post.

Part of Xpressway's success relied on the way in which Russell documented each of its cassettes with detailed, hand-written labels documenting the place and time at which tracks were recorded, giving them an archival quality, as if history was unfolding in the listener's hands. Russell had always been highly organized, having finished a political science degree and been headhunted to do a Masters and teach at the University of Otago in 1984 and 1985, albeit with a blonde mohawk. Shepherd remembered him being 'furiously efficient' when he worked for Flying Nun in Christchurch, organizing their correspondence.[6] This was the network that Russell would draw upon when he started Xpressway. The detail on Xpressway's covers, and Russell's ability to answer letters quickly and send cassettes on time, quickly gained the label a good reputation. It had some big sellers, including the powerful and intimate *The Last Great Challenge in a Dull World* (1990) by Peter Jefferies. Peter collaborated with Russell on Xpressway in the early years, working with musicians and doing some engineering on the releases.

In the 1990s you would never have heard The Dead C on the radio, or on an internet that was still the stuff of science fiction, but you would have read about them in a photocopied zine or seen their name in the Xpressway or other mail order catalogue or zine. Their records were rarely stocked on record shelves but were instead part of a network of mail-order distributors, their catalogues and addresses published in zines and passed from person to person, collector to collector, in Europe, North America, New Zealand and Australia. If you heard The Dead C, it would have been on an album bought through the post or on a dubbed cassette.

The ethos among Siltbreeze and Xpressway artists was not to have a hit record, or be on American college radio, especially since such a thing would have been impossible for the noisy, low-fi recordings that interested Lax and Russell. It was instead to create another economy of listening, one that had integrity and that took place out of sight of an industry that by the late 1980s had become more than awful in its taste in rock music. New Zealand bands trying to make it big more than often than not came home with stories about being unappreciated or ignored by overseas audiences and of being stuffed around by record labels in London and Los Angeles. Chris Knox's attempt to make it big in Sydney with his band Toy Love in 1980, and the stories of The Chills and Straitjacket Fits in London and Los

Angeles have become a part of a national myth around Flying Nun-era bands. After Toy Love, Knox would set the precedent for recording and releasing music without leaving home, famously owning the reel-to-reel recorder that created the iconic Flying Nun sounds of the early 1980s, including The Clean's *Boodle Boodle Boodle*, the *Dunedin Double* compilation, and albums by Knox's own Tall Dwarfs. For The Dead C it was a Tascam porta-studio that saw them through the Siltbreeze years, set up in different places around the musicians as they played into the night on their records of the 1990s.

9 The Port Chalmers Sound

It was Morley's idea to bring Yeats together with Russell to see what they would sound like playing together. This happened in January 1987, and these first jams recalled the early gigs of the late 1970s and early 1980s when people in Dunedin could barely play their instruments. It is not so much that Morley, Russell and Yeats were looking back nostalgically to their experience of these early gigs, but that they carried with them the melancholic knowledge that such times could never occur again. Their interest in recording and releasing records comes from this melancholia, as they do this knowing that they are working in the wake of something, that they are doing something that could not or would not want to be the same. While nostalgia recalls more clearly the past, melancholy describes the acceptance that you can't change the world, that the world will go on doing its thing with or without you. It was not just The Dead C who were experiencing this feeling in Dunedin at the time. Carter remembers that 'Dunedin had changed' upon his return, 'Everyone played free noise ...' that had come to fill some of the void left by the end of the Dunedin Sound scene.[1]

By the mid-1990s The Dead C were playing amidst a new scene of improvising groups dedicated less to playing live than to recording and releasing what they did. These groups represented a shifting array of mostly the same musicians, including Doramaar, Sandoz Lab Technicians, Russell's and

Galbraith's A Handful of Dust, as well as Morley's Gate and his collaboration with Danny Butt, Tanaka-Nixon Meeting as well as the shifting array of the same people playing on Peter Stapleton's Metonymic label.

The groups that came out of this Port Chalmers era modelled themselves on The Dead C's independence. Stapleton was inspired to start Metonymic after Russell's success finding an international audience with Xpressway, while The Dead C stood as local, living examples of how to make and release your own records to an international audience. During the 1990s improvizations in Dunedin, Port Chalmers and Pūrākaunui were recorded and produced using no secret studio techniques and almost no post-production. This coalition of people recording their experiments made up a free noise movement, in a rebellion against the culture of songwriting fostered by Flying Nun in the 1980s, with Stapleton wanting 'to get rid of songs completely' on Metonymic releases.

The drift to improvization in Port Chalmers can be heard on *Clyma*. While it is a rock album, it also slips into noisy moments during which Morley, Russell and Yeats shift sonic gears. 'Electric' is transitional, lying between the song and the improvisation. Coming after 'Sky', Russell and Yeats improvise while Morley recounts lyrics that could easily sit within a more conventional song structure. The track begins with a recording of Maryrose Crook of local band The Renderers, with a heavy New Zealand accent, who is introducing The Dead C and Russell in particular as having slaughtered a pig earlier in preparation for the evening. Morley recites lyrics over the low strum of a guitar and some sharp lines of drumming. Morley's voice is in the low registers against the higher-pitched noise of guitars, amps and white noise that builds into an atmospheric dirge. After a few inaudible lines, he sings 'I'll keep you happy', from Lonnie Mack's blues-gospel tune from 1963, but with more sinister implications. Here Morley might be making a genuine play for love, or something more ambiguous. How could someone make promises from amidst 'Electric''s mash of slowly accelerating noise? Whatever, Morley will soon abandon the chorus as a pulsing chime of feedback sends the relationship of instruments into chaos, before fading into a strumming of electric guitar that takes up the volume of the final minute of the track.

The music for 'Electric' is completely made up on the spot, anticipating the way that in 1996 The Dead C embraced improvisation and abandoned songs altogether. The self-titled *The Dead C* (2000) and *New Electric Music* (2000), on The Dead C's own Language Recordings, reinvent the band with long, experimental dirges and playful, free-jazz-style jams. Songs, if they appear at all, have been entirely invented on the spot, with no rehearsed material to speak of. The 1996 album *Repent* is the first moment at which The Dead C come together in the way we hear them today – as a rock band with no songs, but which plays with rock instruments – but it would be some years before Morley's voice returns to become a part of the total sound of their albums. *Tusk* from 1997, the last of The Dead C's Siltbreeze albums, anticipates this future with a cover taken from a Goya engraving of a person pushing a dagger through the throat of an animal so that it comes back out the mouth like a 'tusk'. The image offers a metaphor for the monstrous shape of Dead C records, that are like night creatures composed from the unconscious. Much of the later Dead C is like 'Head' on *Tusk*, appearing from a noisy mess without quite falling back into this mess, pushing beyond the terrain of sonic disorganization to discover the possibility of a rock music without songs and, in the process, making something poetic.

The Dead C had first tried out the idea of releasing a record without songs, and with material made up on the spot, in *The Operation of the Sonne*, another Siltbreeze record from 1993, just after *Clyma*. Side one was recorded onto a porta-studio, while the second side is a live, improvised gig at The Empire. Its sparse, rangy sounds could well have appeared as one of the live jams being recorded and then released on Corpus Hermeticum and Metonymic. The Dead C's adventures in experimentalism would not be completely smooth. The 1995 album *The White House* is split between dawdling, warbling stoner sounds and three of the most sensational rock tracks that they ever released. After passing through the wobbly feedback, muted drums, and layers of thrashy, unmelodic guitar of 'Voodoo Spell' and 'The New Snow', we arrive at the slow epic 'Your Hand' before turning the album over to hear 'Bitcher', its guitars shifting into a transcendent swirl of sound atop a thrumming of drums, and 'Outside' with a pulsating anthem that disintegrates into an oblong shower of low frequency noise. Here we hear The Dead C at the height of their rock powers, the smoke clearing from a new Dunedin sound culture, finding themselves with a powerful ability to play massively impressive tunes. The album's second half presents their capacity to play together in instrumental synchronicity. *The White House* is split between incredible, sprawling rock themes and the trying out of weird sounds, of working out how far improvization can go.

Reviewer Anthony D'Amico is devastatingly critical of these experimental numbers, calling them 'obnoxious and off-putting', writing that '"Voodoo" literally sounds like two minutes of someone just messing around with a new pedal they bought', while 'The New Snow' 'becomes a near-unlistenable 12-minute spew of masturbatory synth noodling'.[2] *The White House* pulls in two different directions, containing some of The Dead C's greatest rock moments while the band are also wanting to be experimentalists, creating long noise tracks of drones and warbles. This contradiction runs through all The Dead C's material: exceptional tracks recorded on a low-quality porta-studio; total, irreversible changes in drum rhythm; the arrival of a weird, unidentifiable sound just as a song begins to rock out. Rather than trying to seduce the listener, The Dead C's albums more often than not begin with the more alienating tracks, from 'Voodoo Spell' on *The White House* to 'Driver U.F.O.' on *Harsh 70s* and 'Plane' on *Tusk*, not to mention the doubled 'Sunshine/Dirt for Harry' on *Clyma*.

The best of The Dead C happens when the discordance takes place within tracks. In 'Bitcher' on *The White House*, the whine of Morley whistling comes in like a failing police siren atop the downward steps of guitars riffing in slow time. It doesn't sound good on its own, this whistle, but it works in this context. In fact it works more than well, turning a breathy, annoying noise into one part of an enveloping ensemble of sound. Such moments confuse the distinction between noise and rock, experiment and convention. While a flanger works to arc out a stairway of guitar atop chattering drums, the sound of 'Bitcher's' whistle comes on like some Sesame Street kazoo. It briefly offsets the pulsing riff to bring us back from the rock totality and to a sense that what sounds like a mighty, unearthly volume is actually being made by people in a room somewhere. The whistle is a disconcerting but brilliant move, whose unlikely fit with the track opens questions as to how the transcendence of rock music is possible at all, how it is that a few people in a room could be responsible for such affect. On a YouTube rip of 'Bitcher', neil131983 writes that it 'would be far better without that idiot whistling over the top of it'. Yet it is precisely this whistle that creates the dissonance that makes the track what it is; that turns this most unlikely of sounds into something that offsets and adds to the impossibility of The Dead C working as a band at all, that a chaos of instrumentation, of improvisation with rock instruments could somehow pull together into something else, something that holds rock within itself without falling into rock cliché.

The Dead C take questions of quality and turn them around so that the usual, taste making categories of good and bad spin into unrecognizability. At times it is possible to delude oneself into thinking that The Dead C are aiming for a seventh sense, a poetic something that exceeds any particular sound, which offers a way of pulling all their pieces together. This may well be the case, as every band strives for a sensibility that belongs to themselves and nobody else, but there is something else taking place here, that comes not only from the coherence of Russell, Morley and Yeats playing together, but also out of their consistent negation of this coherence, their resistance to being just another rock band, to the format of the song and to the easy seduction of the riff and rhythm into which music all too easily falls. By the time that The Dead C came together in 1987, rock had become a monster as terrible as it was brilliant, a tentacled ogre with the heads of Bon Jovi and Whitesnake, while the local, Flying Nun scene had collapsed beneath the weight of its own pretentions. The Dead C take up their instruments in the aftermath of rock, having recognized its terrible and yet also transcendent possibilities. This historical experience explains something of why, even though they were capable of playing classically epic rock, this was never their aspiration. While tracks like 'Bitcher' on *The White House* and 'World' on *Clyma* are exercises in sonic mastery, they are accompanied by slabs of improvised fuzz or the noodlings of found instrumentation, as The Dead C steer well clear of being mistaken for playing conventional rock music.

As Morley, Russell and Yeats improvised with each other and the people around them, in gigs and late-night sessions that would sometimes turn into albums, they became more comfortable making stuff up as they went along. By the time *Clyma* was recorded they were good at it too, the practice of playing together for more than five years allowing them to develop an intuitive ability to play alongside each other. As Russell says, The Dead C demonstrates that 'you can learn to improvise with a group of people and you can do it as a discipline and you can get good at it.' As they became more confident as improvisers, they got less interested in playing songs. After a tour of the United States in 1995, they decided never to write or compose or play songs again. In America the band felt they had to keep their fans happy by playing songs they would recognize. 'It would be a bit mean', Russell explains, 'to just play a lot of jibbering noise from beginning to end'. But by trying to please the people who had been buying their records, they ended up displeasing themselves. After doing their repertoire over eleven shows in fourteen days, they decided never to do it again. It was a soul-deadening experience and it's one reason why their next, 1996, record is called *Repent*, and is a noisy fuzz of material.

The tour was not the only reason The Dead C had to repent. The title also comes from a deal that Lax, and through him The Dead C, had done with the label Matador and through them Atlantic for distribution, putting the band firmly in the clutches of a major label. The Dead C thought they'd have CDs in chain stores in the US, and still be able to make their own records.

CDs had begun a new era of money-making for record companies, because CDs were cheaper to both manufacture and distribute than vinyl. CD prices were, however, the same as an LP, and the imbalance of cost and price made record companies astounding amounts of money. Not knowing what to do with their cash, bigger labels like Atlantic were making deals with smaller labels like Matador. These labels were, in turn, making manufacturing and distribution deals with tiny, homespun operations like Siltbreeze, who could not believe their luck.

Wanting to get away from the tacky plastic covers that are the bog-standard packaging for CDs, The Dead C asked for digipack covers for *The White House*, that came with full colour printing on the CD as well as the foldout, cardboard cover. And here is where the fine print kicked in. Matador printed 5,000 copies of these and proceeded to charge Lax for warehousing them. The scale of Matador's operations was a complete mismatch for the small runs that Siltbreeze was used to handling. A run of 1,000 was standard for successful bands, while 5,000 was out of the question. The Dead C's next album, *Repent* was named for the regret that came from what should have been a simple commercial arrangement. *Repent* also re-used the digipack cover of *The White House* as packaging, pasting over it with a fading page of photocopied grey paper wrapped around the more expensive product. Tracks are listed from I to VI, minimizing the way in which the cover could be mistaken for marketing the album. *The White House* cover is slightly visible under the cheap photocopy, the band happy to let people know that they were pasting over the cover of their most recent record. Its sound is an assortment of sombre, pulsing gig recordings that lack Morley's vocals, and any pretence to being anything but a documentation of blaring noise. With its improvised, bare cover, *Repent* is one of the band's most commercially unpalatable releases, but also a sonic tour de force.

While *The White House* is a transitional record, *Repent* definitively marks the first release of the second, post-song period of The Dead C, in which the song commodity gives way entirely to something else, to a series of gigs and releases made up on the spot, out of the confidence that Yeats, Russell and Morley now had to pull off something interesting every time they played together. Repent indeed. The new relationship of the sounds of the band to their records can be vexing, as becoming familiar with tracks on later records codes the way that they are heard. On YouTube a song from The Dead C's 2010 gig at the All Tomorrow's Parties festival is called 'South', after a track from the 2010 album *Patience*. The tracks are, however, quite different, including vocals on one and not the other, but the mistake is symptomatic of the way expectation shapes the way we listen to bands, searching out the songs that have come before.

The Dead C's avant-garde dedication to making everything new extends to the re-releases they have been issuing since 2010. As vinyl becomes a thing among collectors seeking more than a streamed listening experience. *Clyma* remained out of print until its re-pressing in 2010 as a double LP, along with a second LP called *Tentative Power* that collects earlier singles. It is part of a slew of re-releases on the North American labels Ba Da Bing! and Jagjaguwar that repackage The Dead C LPs in new ways. The new *Clyma* is not the faithful reproduction of the original release for a discerning collector. One thing missing in the new design is the original sticker (or record label), that on the 1992 *Clyma* featured blocky, black and white images of the band in action. This was Lax's design, from the photographs he took of the band when they were making *Clyma*. On the new release, however, these lovely, analogue images have been replaced by track listings in a Microsoft style of typeface to make them consistent with *Tentative Power*. The whole thing is completely out of time with the original, and not trying to appeal to the nostalgic, Gen X collector (such as myself). Russell's designs for the new Ba Da Bing!/Jagjaguawar re-issues make sure to 'distinguish the various versions clearly. It's a matter of taste, but I am wary of forging my own work'. Again we find this endless renewal, this fear of falling into solipsism, that defines the band's movement, whether this be within an individual track (like 'Sunshine/Dirt for Harry'), on an album (like *The White House*), or in the issuing of albums (as in the *Clyma Est Mort/Tentative Power* release). And solipsism is certainly something rock fans are cursed with. Go no further than Facebook, where Gen Xers post their ten most influential albums that turn up the same post-punk canon of English and North American bands, over and over again. The kind of contrariness that The Dead C have indulged in has long been a way of both resolving themselves into a formidable, noisy trio of anti-musicians and of resisting the problem of nostalgia.

10 The Cells of the Body Return to Their Unliving State

The Dead C's shift into an improvised practice is one that brings up questions around songs, and why the whole mechanism behind listening to music is dominated by them. Why do we listen to the same songs over and over again, whether on albums, on Spotify, or on the radio? One of the best answers to the question came from Sigmund Freud, who argued that people were gripped by repetition-compulsion in which the mind is hard wired to wanting to return to an earlier moment in time, to try and mimic an experience of the past.[1] It's a tempting metaphor for the way the song dominates the consumption of music, becoming a way for the mind to get stuck. After World War One, Freud expanded this idea to explain why European civilization had destroyed itself. Repetition-compulsion had manifested in mass society's embrace of militarism, in a collective fixation, a collective madness, that he proposed came about because of a death drive written into the human body. This is a desire on the part of cells to return to their unliving state, to become the inert matter from which they had arisen. Theodor Adorno was famously more specifically critical of records, of their brevity and the way they fixed performances in time, as a symptom of cultural decline.[2] Freud and Adorno were living in a particularly destructive period of world history, and blamed culture for fostering the violence.

The Dead C also come out of a trenchantly critical view of their own time. As rock music is defined by its opposition to the saccharine experience of pop music, The Dead C put themselves at a distance from rock music that has been hijacked by the music industry. They look back instead to the authenticity and liveness from which rock once came, to the transmission of music in back alley and plantation blues gigs, where music went on all night without repetition. The precedent for Siltbreeze and Xpressway lies in the way blues was recorded in its earliest years, with labels run by enthusiasts rather than professional talent scouts. The Dead C hark back to this moment in rock music's history, when players kept crowds of people bouncing for hours without a written score. Harmonica players, guitarists and vocalists would get to know each other intimately, and bring their special feeling to parties and venues for $5 and an all-night supply of whisky. When record companies started picking star guitarists and singers out of this scene during the 1950s, people like Lightnin' Hopkins and Muddy Waters, they cut the whole culture into identical pieces of acetate and vinyl, requiring a whole industrial apparatus of radio stations, record companies and hi-fi manufacturers to bring them to life.[3] This moment of putting blues on record would pull it into a whole system of power as the printing press had turned writing into empires of administration and law.[4] The immutability of the record made rock stars of musicians, sticking them into time and creating a culture that had become fixated by stuckness, and an industry that would reproduce it and move it across countries and decades.

The Dead C push backwards against this history to reclaim a history of live rock, to work through the trace of this freedom that can still be heard somewhere in the playing of guitars and drums whenever they come together. It's less a nostalgia for this lost moment, than a melancholy that knows there is nothing there to recover, that rock has been defined by its loss of this freedom. The Dead C inhabit this moment of loss, in which everything must begin again and it must begin every time that they play. This is why The Dead C were, from their earliest years, fastidious about recording whatever they did, whether it be jamming at Grey Street or playing to a crowd, because these beginnings could never happen again. It is also why it is impossible to think about The Dead C's albums by any usual measure, why it would be impossible to say, for example, that *Harsh 70s Reality* is better than *Clyma*, because each side of these vinyl LPs begins and begins again in an attempt to clear away what had come before, to simulate an avant-garde originality that contains the moment of its own inspiration.

Morley, Russell and Yeats had, after all, been present at the beginnings of an original movement in rock music in Dunedin in the early 1980s and had seen firsthand the possibilities of originality, of making things anew every time. In the early 1980s, The Clean, The Verlaines and other bands were trying out new material when they gigged at the Empire, trying to impress each other and themselves with their ability not to play music but to concoct it out of nowhere. For the Dunedin Sound bands, the song was the point of originality, it was their creativity at work, yet the song would also condemn these bands to wear out their inspiration in professional studios, overseen by overzealous producers and record companies who sent them on endless tours. The Clean walked away from this future as early as 1982, and The Dead C found their own way around it over the course of the 1990s. They were not the only musicians doing this, not the only people who found other ways of performing and making albums with rock instruments. As a handful of people experimented with new ways of making albums in Port Chalmers, notably released by Russell on his Xpressway and Corpus Hermeticum labels, and Stapleton with Metonymic, they represented a radical alternative to the alternative rock that was rising from the ashes of the 1980s. In North America, Siltbreeze released experiments that drove rock in other avant-garde directions, as magazines like *Bananafish* published interviews, fictocriticism and gibberish to give some context to the scene's gigs and records. The Dead C were not making their work in isolation, but were part of something bigger than themselves, although this bigger was never all that big, patched together with stoned enthusiasm and cynical humour.

The Dead C played into this subaltern geography of spontaneity as they released records in North America, finding an audience that was invisible to them until they toured in 1995. *Clyma* was a joke at the time The Dead C recorded it because they had not found this audience. The titles of the tracks have only ever made sense to Lax and the band:

> Sunshine staggers into Dirt For Harry, intended to take the piss out of one of the Grey Street residents who'd come home one day talking about this new Sun City Girls LP she'd heard called Dirt For Harry. Whuuut? 'You Mean Dawn Of The Devil?' someone asked her. 'Oh,' she said. 'Is that what it's called?' Keeper![5]

And on the Proletariat Idiots release there are scrawls in the grooves, like the graffiti on school desks only meant to be read by the other kids:

> The run off grooves on Side One read 'Beautiful Single Pulse Hell.' Has to be MM; what it means, I can no longer recall. But

I still dig the sentiment. Side Two reads 'Clay Carroll – The Hawk / Where's Porky Now?' Clay Carroll was a relief pitcher for the Cincinnati Reds baseball team in the '70s. His nickname was The Hawk. At work here is a bit of faux Cockney banter. Remember, it's a Fall theme; Clay Carroll came out of Kay Carroll, who was the Fall's manager for many years. I know, fascinating. The Clay Carroll thing was all me. Those guys had no idea what the fuck I was on about. But at that point, it was all a big hoot. Let it ride.

'Where's Porky Now?' is a reference to Porky Prime, the legendary lacquer cutter/audio engineer who used to inscribe in the runoff grooves he worked on 'Another Porky Prime Cut.' It's a tribute to Porky, Rough Trade, The Fall, Pere Ubu, all of those who sailed before who had made a band like Dead C possible and a piker like me to believe in them.[6]

The joke at the heart of *Clyma* is that its parody, its self-deprecating imitation of live albums is also a commitment to staying out of the way of the bullshit that more often than not drives music and its pretentions. The record itself is part of an ongoing experiment in what makes rock work, but the experiment can't take itself too seriously or it becomes the very thing it is trying to avoid. As the screech of an amplifier cuts into a chunky riff on the guitar, or a drum fill arrives amidst what seemed to be a tune on its way somewhere, The Dead C play a game with what is expected of them as a rock band. It is a game that they play with each other as much as with their audience.

After the epic 'World', in which The Dead C concoct a slow, tidal symphony of rock brilliance, the band return to the trouble that they want to make for themselves and for music in *Clyma*'s final track 'Das Fluten, Das Fluten (Oh Mama I can't Go)'.

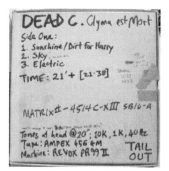

Figures 5 and 6 *The reel-to-reel tapes destined for America. Photos Tom Lax.*

There's no way to swing your arms to this number, as the instruments overlay each other like some abstract Japanese acoustic free-jazz piece, and a guitar is made to sound like the inside of a piano while drums roll occasionally as if to introduce a rhythm that never arrives. Lax recalls:

> Das Fluten, Das Fluten (Oh Mama I Can't Go) has flutes on it, so there you go. This was a Bruce Russell knee-slapper. It has something to do with Captain Beefheart shouting 'The Blimp, the blimp!' and then muttering 'Oh mama, I can't go.' Pull your copy of Trout Mask Replica, spin the track and you'll hear what I mean. Blimp was changed to Flute, then Fluten, then Das Fluten, as the German language title 'theme' was now so quixotically amusing. Get it? Or are those tears streaming down your cheeks belying another interpretation?[7]

It's as if, after 'World' has shaken the record into the zone of making classic, voluminous rock, the band lose interest and want to try something else for a change, to twiddle their instruments again rather than getting carried away by some fantasy of being rock musicians.

'Das Fluten' is a sparse recording of guitar warbling, spikes of drumming, a low thrum of machine noise and yes, the sound of flutes. There is some confusion around the origins of these bamboo instruments that were lying around at Grey Street. Russell thought they may have been left there by Sandoz Lab Technicians, who were part of the new improvised sound scene that had arisen in town by this time, and who use flutes alongside many other found instruments on *Synaptic Acres* (1999). Morley, however, thinks that they were his, and it may be that he was thinking about using them on Gate or any number of other music projects he was developing. In any case, another superb Morley guitar riff holds the track together, leading Yeats's drums along with an increased pace and rhythm, while Russell switches from screeching a flute he has found somewhere to chaotic guitar. It's almost as if having achieved as much synchrony as they ever will with 'World', the band make sure to disassemble into component pieces, to find their individualism again in the sharp focus of clearly defined sounds. As the track winds to a close, Russell pushes the low hum into the foreground by changing its pitch up and down, while Yeats paces his beat into nothingness. The sound of scattered applause is blatantly cut into the last seconds of the record, in a final, tongue-in-cheek play upon the album's liveness. Stolen from a recording of a Renderers gig that someone found lying around, it is a slim choice for a crowd recording. If this is an attempt to simulate a live gig, it's a hilarious and desultory effort. In an attempt to make music in an age that has destroyed music's freedom, they resort to what Lax calls a 'cornball' humour, yet *Clyma* is also a sincere document of dissatisfaction with the way rock music is typically played.[8] Throwing things together to see if they can make a band that sounds different to other bands, The Dead C tear apart the pretensions of musicians trying to write the perfect song, play the perfect beat, and secure their place in popular culture. They play, instead, in charred, noisy anticipation of what might come after the capitalist apocalypse, while knowing that this end is not likely to come.

Clyma ultimately captures something of the mood of those living at the bottom of the Western economic world in the 1990s. After the cocaine snorting heights of the 1980s had collapsed into financial doldrums and the music industry was making new balloons of profit from cheaply manufactured CDs, the twentieth century appeared to have little else to offer. *Clyma*'s humour comes from a cynicism born not only from this historical moment, but also from its musicians having witnessed the heights of rock music come and go in Dunedin. This is not a cynical record, however. Morley elevates the instrumental chaos with staunch and poetic lyrics, while the sheer energy of the performances on *Clyma* betray a belief in the transformational power of rock, as does the do-it-yourself ethos that inspired it, the big-headed belief that a great record could be made with a port-a-cam and a good time. In this way The Dead C offer insights into the dynamics of rock that need not be produced out of the stressful world of studios and stadium-style performances, the sense that one band can do better than another. Morley, Russell and Yeats veer instead into territory that they have invented as their own, stumbling into a sound that is unmistakably The Dead C. The tension between a marching drum beat and a screeching amplifier, a noodling guitar and a bamboo flute, pushes and fills out the spectrum of what it is possible for a band to do without losing a sense of itself. 'The trip is everything', says Russell, a trip that teeters on not being rock music at all but chaos and noise, for the trip is not only everything but about finding the way back to nothing, about overcoming the pretentions of rock by pushing outward to see how far it might go before falling apart. It does not always make sense, and not everyone will make sense out of it, but when the three stubborn instrumentalists create something out of that nether zone between rock and noise, it invariably appears as if by accident. Suspended somewhere between songs and improvisations, wilfulness, and playfulness, *Clyma* is a blistering live record made in a home studio, a serious excursion into the mists of rock music while taking the piss, a classic New Zealand album made at the bullish insistence of an enthusiastic American fan.

Notes

Chapter 1

1 Nick Cain, '"I know more about taking a shit than I do about music" The Dead C' (1995) in *Archive Fever: New Zealand Noise Music Fanzine Interviews 1991–2002*, ed. Noel Meek, Marhaug Forlag, Oslo, 2002, n.p.

2 Rob Elba (host), *That Record Got Me High*: 'S5E193 – The Dead C – *'Trapdoor Fucking Exit'* with Joe Tunis' season 5, episode 193, 6 November 2021. Available at: www.thatrecordgotme high.com/s5e193-the-dead-c-trapdoor-fucking-exit-with-joe-tunis/.

3 Tom Lax, 'Corresponding with NZ'. *Everybody Knows this is Nowhere*, no 1 (2013): 16.

4 Nick Cain, Alastair Galbraith and Bruce Russsell, 'A Chat with Bruce Russell and Alastair Galbraith of A Handful of Dust at The Stomach on Friday 15 September 1995', in *Archive Fever: New Zealand Noise Music Fanzine Interviews 1991–2002*, ed. Noel Meek, Marhaug Forlag, Oslo, 2002, n.p.

5 Graeme Jefferies, *Time Flowing Backwards: A Memoir*, Mosaic Press, Oakville, Canada, 2018, p 283.

6 Joe Tunis (host), *My Teeth Need Attention*: 'Episode 16 – Tom Lax interview', 18 February 2022. Available at: www.myteethneedattention.com/.

7 Tom Lax, 'Cowbell Need Not Apply: The Story Behind the Making of the Dead C's *Clyma Est Mort*', *Volcanic Tongue*, 2010. Available at: https://web.archive.org/web/20160425032403/http://volcanictongue.co.uk/columns/show/15.

8 Roger Shepherd, *In love with these times: My life with Flying Nun Records*, Harper Collins, Auckland, 2016, p 174.

9 Shayne Carter, *Dead people I Have Known*, Victoria University Press, Wellington, 2019, p 249.

10 See Alex Parrish, 'Talking Noise: An Interview w/Michael Morley (of Gate & The Dead C), *Monster Fresh* 27 August, 2010. Available at: www.monsterfresh.com/2010/08/27/michael-morley-interview-dead-c-gate/; and Roland Woodbe, 'Dead C–Harsh 70's Reality–20th anniversary Edition–OUT NOW!,' *Siltblog* 23 August, 2012. Available at: http://siltblog.blogspot.com/2012/08/dead-c-harsh-70s-reality-20th.html.

11 Tom Lax, 'Cowbell Need Not Apply.'

12 Nick Cain, '"I know more about taking a shit than I do about music."'

Chapter 2

1 The late Dunedin musician Peter Gutteridge, of Snapper and co-writer of The Clean's 'Point that Thing' heckled the band with this apt piece of insight at a Dead C gig around 1992. In Bruce Russell with Jordan N Mamone, 'In Praise of Miscompetence: Noise Icons the Dead C Remain Mysterious as Ever,' *Observer Music*, 15 September 2016. Available at: https://observer.com/2016/09/in-praise-of-miscompetence-noise-icons-the-dead-c-remain-mysterious-as-ever/.

2 Greg Freeman, 'The Noise of the Food Falling from the Beaks of the Sacred Chickens.' *Bananafish* 6 (August 1991), n.p.

3 Alastair Galbraith, 'Preface: A quarter of a century of noise?/ Kill me now!', in *Left-handed Blows: Writing on Sound 1993–2009*, ed. Bruce Russell, Clouds, Auckland, 2009, n.p.

4 See *The Chills: The Triumph & Tragedy of Martin Phillips* (documentary), dir. Julia Parnell, Notable Pictures and Fire Films, New Zealand, 2019.

5 The published versions of 'What is Free?' are scarce on the ground, but the full text is easily found with an internet search. For the bibliophiles among you, someone has generously uploaded the Gate CD insert onto the Discogs page of the release, listed as *I.O.M. (1967–1992)* from 1992. It was then published in *Bananafish* no 7 (1993), 10–12; in *Logopandocy: The Journal of Vain Erudition* 1, no 2 (October 1994): 2–7 that came with A Handful of Dust, *Musica Humana* on Corpus Hermeticum (Hermes 005) and in Bruce Russell, *Left-handed Blows: Writing on Sound 1993–2009*, Clouds, Auckland, 2009, 21–24.

6 See Bruce Russell, 'Left-handed Blows: Towards a Technique of Incognito', in *Left-handed Blows: Writing on Sound 1993–2009*, Clouds, Auckland, 2009, pp. 1–17 at 3; Bruce Russell, 'Towards a Social Ontology of Improvised Sound Work', in *Noise and Capitalism*, ed. Anthony Iles, Gipuzkoako Foru Aldundia – Arteleku, San Sebastian, 2009, pp. 73–95; Bruce Russell, '"Antique Bird-like Chatter": Mis-Competence in New Zealand Electronic Music', *SoundBleed*, 25 September 2013. Available at: https://soundbleedjournal.wordpress.com/2013/09/25/antique-bird-like-chatter-mis-competence-in-new-zealand-electronic-music-bruce-russell/; and 'What True Project Has Been Lost?': Towards a Social Ontology of Improvised Sound Work, PhD dissertation, RMIT University, Melbourne, 2016.

7 Bruce Russell, 'Too Reel,' *Landfall* no 219, 2010, p 105.

Chapter 3

1 Russell, 'What True Project Has Been Lost?'

2 Guy Debord, Society of the Spectacle, Black and Red, Detroit, 1973.

3 Shepherd, *In Love with These Times,* p. 174; The Dead C at Chippendale House in *The Various Artistes: Dead C, Plagal Grind, Sun Series, This Kind of Punishment, Chris Knox.* video. 8 August, 1987. Nga Taonga Sound & Vision item number F84827.

4 Redmer Yska, 'LSD: New Zealand's LSD History', *Matters of Substance* 28, no 1, 1 March 2017. Available at: www. drugfoundation.org.nz/matters-of-substance/archive/ march-2017/lsd-new-zealands-lsd-history/.

5 Bruce Russell, '1981: Godzone's Freaked-out Year Zero', liner notes for *Time to Go – The Southern Psychedelic Moment: 1981– 1986* (2XLP), Flying Nun, New Zealand, 2012.

6 Carter, *Dead People I Have Known*, p. 250

7 Lax, 'Cowbell Need Not Apply.'

8 Lax, 'Cowbell Need Not Apply.'

Chapter 4

1 Lax, 'Cowbell Need Not Apply.'

2 Nick Cain, Bruce Russell, Michael Morley and Robbie Yeats, 'Invisible Jukebox: The Dead C', *The Wire* no 278 (April 2007), pages unknown.

3 Mark Fisher, 'Memorex for the Krakens: The Fall's Pulp Modernism,' Parts I–III, 2007, k-punk blog. Available at: http:// k-punk.abstractdynamics.org/archives/2007_02.html.

4 Least of all Roger Shepherd. See Shepherd, *In Love With These Times,* 103–112.

5 On Smith's tendency to sabotage his career, see Paul Hanley, *Have a Bleedin Guess: The Story of Hex Enduction Hour*, Route, Pontefract, 2020, especially pp 172–175.

6 This was the case for Siltbreeze's first two releases, Halo of Flies's *Richie's Dog* (1989) and The Dead C's *Helen Said This/Bury* (1990). In Tunis, 'Episode 16 – Tom Lax interview'.

7 Lax, 'Cowbell Need Not Apply.'

8 Andrew Schmidt, 'The Stones,' *Audioculture / Iwi Waiata*, 5 December, 2013. Available at: www.audioculture.co.nz/profile/the-stones.

9 In Nigel Benson, 'Hey You, Get off our Cloud,' *Otago Daily Times*, 2 April 2022, Available at: www.odt.co.nz/news/dunedin/hey-you-get-our-cloud.

10 Matthew Bannister, *Positively George Street: Sneaky Feelings and the Dunedin Sound – A Personal Reminiscence*, Reed, Auckland, 1999, p 57.

Chapter 5

1 In Schmidt, 'The Stones.'

2 David Keenan, 'Honour without Profit,' *The Wire* 353 (July 2013): 27–34 at 30.

3 'Local Bands: The Clean,' *Radio Times*, 1982, n.p.

4 Andrew Schmidt, 'The Clean Part One 1978–1988,' *Audio Culture: The Noisy Library of New Zealand Music*. Available at: www.audioculture.co.nz/people/the-clean/stories/the-clean-part-one-1978-1988

5 'Local Bands' n.p.

6 Lax, 'Corresponding with NZ.'

7 See Graeme Downes, 'The Clean: Modal Conflict and Resolution,' *Music in New Zealand* 16 (1992): 21–23 at 23. On his own songwriting, see Downes, 'Songwriting Process in the Verlaines' Album *Corporate Moronic*, *Dunedin Soundings: Place*

and *Performance*, ed. Dan Bendrups and Graeme Downes, Otago University Press, Dunedin, 2011, pp 43–56.

8 In Keenan, 'Honour without Profit', p 30.

9 Andrew Schmidt, 'The Verlaines', *Audioculture / Iwi Waiata*, 4 February, 2021. Available at: www.audioculture.co.nz/profile/the-verlaines.

10 Schmidt, 'The Verlaines'.

11 Keenan, 'Honour without profit', p. 29.

12 Gary Steel, 'Dunedin Story', in *The Dunedin Sound: Some Disenchanted Evening*, ed. Ian Chapman, David Bateman Ltd, Auckland, 2016, 152-155 at 154.

13 Steel, 'Dunedin Story', 154.

14 David Eggleton, *Ready to Fly*, Craig Patton, Nelson, 2003, 114.

Chapter 6

1 In Nick Cain, 'Hated in the Nation: The Dead C. Vs New Zealand', liner notes for The Dead C, *The Dead C. Perform Vain, Erudite and Stupid, Selected Works: 1987–2005* (bing050), CD, 2006.

2 In Keenan, 'Honour without Profit', p. 28.

3 Carter, *Dead people I have known*, p. 187.

4 Bruce Russell and Marco Fusinato, 'Poi$son + Lie$ = Money + Death – The Axe Interview', in *Left Handed Blows: Writing on Sound: 1993–2009*, ed. Bruce Russell, Clouds, Auckland, 2009, pp 51–60 at 55.

5 Cain, '"I know more about taking a shit than I do about music"', n.p.

6 Shepherd, *In Love with these times*, p. 187.

Chapter 7

1 Gary Steel, 'Dunedin Story', p. 154.
2 Morley in Parrish, 'Talking Noise'.
3 Neil Young, *Waging Heavy Peace: A Hippie Dream*, Blue Rider Press, New York, 2012, chapter 64, ebook.
4 Jean Baudrillard, 'The Conspiracy of Art'. in *The Conspiracy of Art*, trans Ames Hodges, Semiotext(e), New York, 2005, pp 25–29.
5 Agnes Gayraud, *Dialectic of Pop*, trans Robin Mackay, Daniel Miller and Nina Power, Urbanomic, Falmouth, 2019, p 18.

Chapter 8

1 Tunis, 'Episode 16 – Tom Lax Interview'. See also Tony Rettman (host), *Sandpaper Lullaby*: 'Podcast #1: Tom Lax (Siltbreeze Records), 27 January 2020. Available at: https://rettman.substack.com/p/sandpaper-lullaby-podcast-1-tom-lax#details.
2 Russell in Cain, Galbraith and Russell, 'A Chat with Bruce Russell and Alastair Galbraith of A Handful of Dust at The Stomach on Friday 15 September 1995.'
3 Tom Lax, Interview with Tony Rettman, *Sandpaper Lullaby*, Tom Lax, Interview with Joe Tunis.
4 Carter, *Dead People I Have Known*, p. 246.
5 Carter, *Dead People I Have Known*, p. 246.
6 Shepherd, *In Love With These Times,* p. 174.

Chapter 9

1 Carter, *Dead People I Have Known*, p. 284. Free noise is typically the way these albums are historicized, rather than as belonging to the Port Chalmers scene, since many of the best improvised, experimental and noise albums come from elsewhere in the country. For an introduction see Peter Stapleton, 'Periphery to Centre: Dunedin Noise in the Late 1990s', in *Erewhon Calling: Experimental sound in New Zealand*, ed. Bruce Russell with Richard Francis and The Audio Foundation, Audio Foundation, Wellington, 2012, pp. 108–113; and Jon Dale, '90s New Zealand Free Noise', *Shfl*. Available at: https://theshfl.com/guide/NZ-free-noise.

2 Anthony D'Amico, Review of The Dead C, *The White House*, 15 February 2015. Available at: www.brainwashed.com/index.php?option=com_content&view=article&id=10358:the-dead-c-qthe-white-houseq&catid=13:albums-and-singles&Itemid=133.

Chapter 10

1 Sigmund Freud, *Beyond the Pleasure Principle*, trans CJM Hubback, *The International Psycho-analytical Press*, London, 1922.

2 Theodor W Adorno, 'The Form of the Phonograph Record', October 55 (Winter 1990): 56–61.

3 Bruno Latour, 'Drawing Things Together', in *Representation in Scientific Practice*, eds M. Lynch and S. Woolgar, MIT Press, Cambridge, MA, 1990, pp 19–68.

4 See Benedict Anderson, *Imagined Communities: Reflections on the Origin and Spread of Nationalism*, revised edition, Routledge, Abingdon, 2017.

5 Lax, 'Cowbell Need Not Apply'.

6 Lax, 'Cowbell Need Not Apply'. As my editor Jon Dale points out, the reference here might also be to a 1978 Television Personalities single, *Where's Bill Grundy Now?*

7 Lax, 'Cowbell Need Not Apply'.

8 Lax, 'Cowbell Need Not Apply'.

References

Adorno, Theodor W. 'The Form of the Phonograph Record', *October* 55 (Winter 1990): 56–61.

Anderson, Benedict, *Imagined Communities: Reflections on the origin and spread of nationalism*, revised edition, Routledge, Abingdon, 2017.

Bannister, Matthew, *Positively George Street: Sneaky Feelings and the Dunedin Sound – A personal reminiscence*, Reed, Auckland, 1999.

Baudrillard, Jean, 'The Conspiracy of Art', in *The Conspiracy of Art*, trans. Ames Hodges, Semiotext(e), New York, 2005, pp. 25–29.

Benson, Nigel, 'Hey You, Get off our Cloud', *Otago Daily Times*, 2 April 2022. Available at: www.odt.co.nz/news/dunedin/hey-you-get-our-cloud

Cain, Nick, '"I know more about taking a shit than I do about music" The Dead C' (1995), in *Archive Fever: New Zealand Noise Music Fanzine Interviews 1991–2002*, ed. Noel Meek, Marhaug Forlag, Oslo, 2002, n.p.

Cain, Nick, 'Hated in the Nation: The Dead C. Vs New Zealand', liner notes for The Dead C, *The Dead C. Perform Vain, Erudite and Stupid, Selected Works: 1987–2005* (bing050), CD, 2006.

Cain, Nick, Alastair Galbraith and Bruce Russell, 'A Chat with Bruce Russell and Alastair Galbraith of A Handful of Dust at The Stomach on Friday 15 September 1995', in *Archive Fever: New Zealand Noise Music Fanzine Interviews 1991–2002*, ed. Noel Meek, Marhaug Forlag, Oslo, 2002, n.p.

Cain, Nick, Bruce Russell, Michael Morley and Robbie Yeats, 'Invisible Jukebox: The Dead C', *The Wire* no. 278 (April 2007), pages unknown.

Carter, Shayne, *Dead people I have known*, Victoria University Press, Wellington, 2019.

D'Amico, Anthony, Review of The Dead C, *The White House*, 15 February 2015. Available at: www.brainwashed.com/index.php?option=com_content&view=article&id=10358:the-dead-c-qthe-white-houseq&catid=13:albums-and-singles&Itemid=133.

Dale, Jon, '90s New Zealand Free Noise', *Shfl*, https://theshfl.com/guide/NZ-free-noise.

Debord, Guy, *Society of the Spectacle*, Black and Red, Detroit, 1970.

Downes, Graeme, 'The Clean: Modal Conflict and Resolution', *Music in New Zealand* 16 (1992): 21–23.

Downes, Graeme, 'Songwriting Process in the Verlaines' album *Corporate Moronic*', *Dunedin Soundings: Place and Performance*, ed. Dan Bendrups and Graeme Downes, Otago University Press, Dunedin, 2011, 43–56.

Eggleton, David, *Ready to Fly*, Craig Patton, Nelson, 2003.

Elba, Rob (host), *That Record Got Me High*: 'S5E193 –The Dead C – "*Trapdoor Fucking Exit*" with Joe Tunis' season 5, episode 193, 6 November, 2021. Available at: www.thatrecordgotmehigh.com/s5e193-the-dead-c-trapdoor-fucking-exit-with-joe-tunis/

Fisher, Mark, 'Memorex for the Krakens: The Fall's pulp modernism,' parts I – III, 2007, k-punk blog. Available at: http://k-punk.abstractdynamics.org/archives/2007_02.html.

Freeman, Greg, 'The Noise of the Food Falling from the Beaks of the Sacred Chickens', *Bananafish* 6 (August 1991), n.p.

Freud, Sigmund, *Beyond the Pleasure Principle*, trans. C.J.M. Hubback, The International Psycho-analytical Press, London, 1922.

Galbraith, Alastair, 'Preface: A quarter of a century of noise?/ Kill me now!', in *Left-handed blows: Writing on sound 1993–2009*, ed. Bruce Russell, Clouds, Auckland, 2009, n.p.

Gayraud, Agnes, *Dialectic of Pop*, trans Robin Mackay, Daniel Miller and Nina Power, Urbanomic, Falmouth, 2019.

Hanley, Paul, *Have a Bleedin Guess: The Story of Hex Enduction Hour*, Route, Pontefract, 2020.

Jefferies, Graeme, *Time Flowing Backwards: A Memoir*, Mosaic Press, Oakville, Canada, 2018.

Keenan, David, 'Honour without Profit', *The Wire* 353 (July 2013): 27–34.

Latour, Bruce, 'Drawing Things Together', in *Representation in Scientific Practice*, eds M. Lynch and S. Woolgar, MIT Press, Cambridge, MA, 1990, pp. 19–68.

Lax, Tom, 'Corresponding with NZ', *Everybody Knows this is Nowhere*, no 1 (2013): 15–18.

Lax, Tom, 'Cowbell Need Not Apply: The story behind the making of the Dead C's *Clyma Est Mort*', *Volcanic Tongue*, 2010. Available at: https://web.archive.org/web/20160425032403/ http://volcanictongue.co.uk/columns/show/15

'Local Bands: The Clean', *Radio Times,* 1982, n.p.

Parrish, Alex, 'Talking Noise: An Interview w/Michael Morley (of Gate & The Dead C), *Monster Fresh* 27 August, 2010. Available at: www.monsterfresh.com/2010/08/27/michael-morley-interview-dead-c-gate/.

Rettman, Tony (host), *Sandpaper Lullaby*: 'Podcast #1: Tom Lax (Siltbreeze Records), 27 January 2020. Available at: https://

rettman.substack.com/p/sandpaper-lullaby-podcast-1-tom-lax#details.

Russell, Bruce, 'What True Project Has Been Lost?': Towards a social ontology of improvised sound work, PhD dissertation, RMIT University, Melbourne, 2016.

Russell, Bruce, '"Antique Bird-like Chatter": Mis-Competence in New Zealand Electronic Music', *SoundBleed*, 25 September 2013. Available at: https://soundbleedjournal.wordpress.com/2013/09/25/antique-bird-like-chatter-mis-competence-in-new-zealand-electronic-music-bruce-russell/.

Russell, Bruce, '1981: Godzone's freaked-out year zero', liner notes for *Time to Go – The Southern Psychedelic Moment: 1981–1986* (2XLP), Flying Nun, New Zealand, 2012.

Russell, Bruce, 'Left-handed Blows: Towards a Technique of Incognito', in *Left-handed Blows: Writing on Sound 1993–2009*, Clouds, Auckland, 2009, pp 1–17.

Russell, Bruce, 'Too reel', *Landfall* no. 219, 2010, pp. 98–106.

Russell, Bruce, 'Towards a Social Ontology of Improvised Sound Work', in *Noise and Capitalism*, ed. Anthony Iles, Gipuzkoako Foru Aldundia – Arteleku, San Sebastian, 2009, pp 73–95.

Russell, Bruce, 'What is Free?' *Bananafish* no 7 (1993), 10–12. Re-published in *Logopandocy: The Journal of Vain Erudition* 1, no 2 (October 1994): 2–7 and *Left-handed Blows: Writing on Sound 1993–2009*, Clouds, Auckland, 2009, 21–24.

Russell, Bruce and Marco Fusinato, 'Poi$son + Lie$ = Money + Death – The Axe Interview', in *Left Handed Blows: Writing on Sound: 1993–2009*, ed. Bruce Russell, Clouds, Auckland, 2009, pp 51–60.

Russell, Bruce with Jordan N. Mamone, 'In Praise of Miscompetence: Noise Icons the Dead C Remain Mysterious as Ever,' *Observer Music*, 15 September 2016. Available at: https://observer.com/2016/09/in-praise-of-miscompetence-noise-icons-the-dead-c-remain-mysterious-as-ever/.

Schmidt, Andrew, 'The Clean Part One 1978–1988', *Audio Culture: The Noisy Library of New Zealand Music*. Available at: www.audioculture.co.nz/people/the-clean/stories/the-clean-part-one-1978-1988.

Schmidt, Andrew, 'The Stones,' *Audioculture / Iwi Waiata*, 5 December, 2013. Available at: www.audioculture.co.nz/profile/the-stones.

Shepherd, Roger, *In Love with These Times: My Life with Flying Nun Records*, Harper Collins, Auckland, 2016.

Stapleton, Peter, 'Periphery to Centre: Dunedin Noise in the Late 1990s', in *Erewhon Calling: Experimental Sound in New Zealand*, ed. Bruce Russell with Richard Francis and The Audio Foundation, Audio Foundation, Wellington, 2012, pp 108–113.

Steel, Gary, 'Dunedin Story', in *The Dunedin Sound: Some Disenchanted Evening*, ed. Ian Chapman, David Bateman Ltd, Auckland, 2016, 152–155.

The Chills: The Triumph & Tragedy of Martin Phillips (documentary), dir. Julia Parnell, Notable Pictures and Fire Films, New Zealand, 2019.

'The Various Artistes: Dead C, Plagal Grind, Sun Series, This Kind of Punishment, Chris Knox.' video. 8 September, 1987. Nga Taonga Sound & Vision item number F84827.

Tunis, Joe (host), *My Teeth Need Attention*: 'Episode 16 – Tom Lax interview', 18 February 2022. Available at: www.myteethneedattention.com/.

Woodbe, Ronald, 'Dead C – Harsh 70's Reality – 20th anniversary Edition-OUT NOW!,' *Siltblog* 23 August, 2012. Available at:

http://siltblog.blogspot.com/2012/08/dead-c-harsh-70s-reality-20th.html.

Young, Neil, *Waging Heavy Peace: A Hippie Dream*, Blue Rider Press, New York, 2012, ebook.

Yska, Redmer, 'LSD: New Zealand's LSD History', *Matters of Substance* 28, no 1, 1 March 2017. Available at: www.drugfoundation.org.nz/matters-of-substance/archive/march-2017/lsd-new-zealands-lsd-history/.

Index

Bands and people

Companies, labels, zines and magazines

Places true and invented